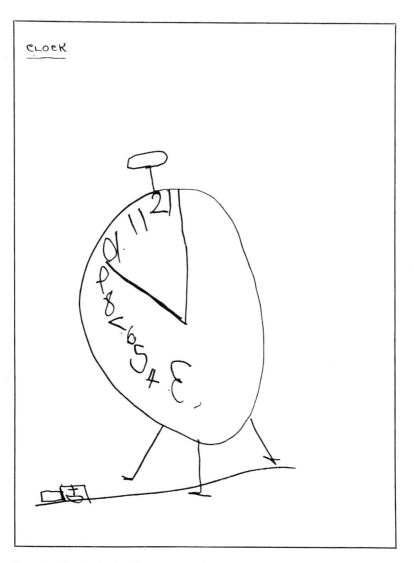

Drawing of a clock, showing severe spatial difficulties, neglect of the right half of the dial, and various rotations and reversals.

The child was an intelligent boy of 6 years 8 months with a family history of dyslexia. Seen again at the age of 9 years and 1 month, his reading and spelling ages were at a 7-year level. His spontaneous drawing of a clock was then well executed.

Frontispiece

The Dyslexic Child
(being the 2nd and augmented Edition of Developmental Dyslexia)

Macdonald Critchley

Consulting Physician, National Hospital, Queen Square, London
President, World Federation of Neurology

William Heinemann Medical Books Limited
London

First Edition 1964
Reprinted 1965
Reprinted 1967
Second Edition 1970
Reprinted 1972

ISBN 0 433 06700 4

Reproduced and Printed in Great Britain by
Redwood Press Limited, Trowbridge & London

Contents

Preface

This volume represents a revised and much expanded version of "Developmental Dyslexia" which was published in 1964.

More and more attention is currently paid to mal-achievements in the scholastic curriculum—so well described in *Alice in Wonderland* as "Reeling and writhing, and the different branches of arithmetic—ambition, distraction, uglification and derision. Mysteries, ancient and modern, with seaography. Drawling, stretching and fainting in coils. Laughing and Grief." We are particularly concerned with defects of the first named, what Lewis Carrol shrewdly dubbed "reeling". Our problem is that of Somerset Maugham's illiterate verger who confessed . . . "the cook in my first place tried to teach me to read, but I didn't seem to have the knack for it. I couldn't seem able to get the letters in me 'ead when I was a nipper."

Since the appearance in 1964 of the first edition entitled *Development Dyslexia* many important events have taken place within the province of reading retardation. The World Federation of Neurology, having constituted a Research Group with an international membership, have come up with an agreed definition of developmental dyslexia. Critics had hitherto reproached neurologists with being unwilling to define their problem, if indeed they were capable of doing so. In London, the Word Blind Centre is giving valuable aid to very many unfortunate dyslexics, and is also carrying out a study into such problems as the nature of dyslexia, its clinical diversities and its method or methods of remediation. The Centre has also embarked upon the instruction of teachers and others who are concerned with children who are tardy in learning to read. Throughout Great Britain "pressure groups" have been founded in many regions, where all those interested in this problem—whether doctors, parents, teachers, or psychologists—can meet and discuss these pressing difficulties.

In other countries problems of dyslexia are now showing themselves as a topical, even urgent, subject of concern to educators, legislators, and parents. Many symposia have been held with dyslexia as the key topic. In some American states, particularly Texas, Washington, and Connecticut, the special remedial teaching of children with reading-problems, has formed an important plank in the legislative platform. At a Federal level, Congress in 1969 ear-marked 79 million dollars for the education of handicapped children, and in the same year a bill was introduced into the Senate by Senator Yarborough (Texas) with the entitlement "Children with Learning Disability". Congressman Perkins (Kentucky) put up a similar bill to the House of Representatives. Dyslexic children are included within this particular category.

Outside the English-speaking world the pace has been almost as rapid. Special discussions upon this subject have been held in Vienna, and, largely stimulated by the World Federation of Neurology, work has been forging ahead in France, Belgium, Germany, Latin America, Spain, Czechoslovakia, Bulgaria, Roumania, Taiwan; as well as France and Belgium.

Less often nowadays do we hear of teachers snidely proclaiming an ignorance of the problem of dyslexia, nor of educationalists casting doubts as to its very existence. These two nihilistic attitudes are becoming things of the past.

Much remains to be done, however, "The foundation of knowledge must be laid by reading" as Johnson proclaimed. We cannot afford to tolerate within our economy a nub of intelligent stable individuals who plod through life intellectually deprived. The sum total of teachers skilled in training dyslexics is all too small. Facilities for remedial training are still grossly inadequate. From the scientific point of view many topics for further scrutiny have emerged, clamouring for long-term research.

This present volume, based upon the monograph published five years ago adds information selected from the recent literature. More particularly, the study is based upon a series of 620 subjects, all personally examined, who were referred to me as possible cases of word-blindness. Not all of these children turned out to be true instances of developmental dyslexia, but the majority were found to fall within that diagnostic category.

In preparing this volume I would like to acknowledge with gratitude the shrewd and unstinting assistance afforded me by Mrs. E. Hargreaves; and also the back-room expertise of Mrs. J. Robertson whose chore it was to type and retype the manuscript.

October 1969   M. C.

Introduction

The "discovery" of congenital word-blindness just over 65 years ago was a notable event in medical taxonomy. For the next few decades a series of important contributions betray the interest which this idea had aroused in medical circles, first in Great Britain, then in Europe and later still in North America. Despite changes in terminology, the attitudes towards this disability became firmly established. Of late, however, the situation has changed. The word "congenital word-blindness" was now dropped out of scientific literature in favour of "developmental, or specific dyslexia". The problem began to show signs of ceasing to be regarded as a medical issue at all, while other disciplines, such as pedagogy and psychology, assumed a more active and even aggressive role.

The results of this changed orientation in thinking were both unexpected and unfortunate. When neurologists demarcated "congenital word-blindness' as an entity, they did not for a moment intend to embrace the whole community of illiterates, semi-illiterates, poor readers, slow readers, retarded readers, bad spellers, or reluctant writers. That was a problem which lay outside their sphere of influence, and furthermore only remotely concerned the distinctive cases of constitutional disability in which they as neurologists were interested.

A number of educational psychologists both in this country and in the U.S.A. began to enter the scene, only to obscure the issue at times. Many of these—though certainly not all—regarded the problem of difficulty in learning to read as forming what they called a "continuum": something which ranged from intellectual inadequacy at one end of the scale, to neurosis at the other. This latter, it was alleged, may be the product of such unpropitious environmental factors as broken homes, drunken parents, teacher-pupil hostility, absenteeism, and so on. Many educationalists appear sceptical as to whether developmental dyslexia occurs at all; some go further and proclaim outright that it is a myth. Others say that it might exist, but they have never seen it; or, that they are familiar enough with it, but that it is a psychologically determined illness: or else a manifestation of mental defect: or perhaps the result of starting a child's reading lessons too early; or too late; or of employing wrong techniques: or else it is the price we pay in England for our illogical spelling. So the blame has fallen upon one scapegoat after another, the teacher, the parents, and the child. Even among medical writers there has also been some confused thinking on occasions, for it has been hinted that dyslexia might have something to do with birth trauma: or even with the mother having had more children than was good for her.

The practical upshot of all these muddled ideas of multiple aetiology has been an unfortunate lack of any consistent policy to help the majority of these unhappy victims of dyslexia.

Another instance of illogical argument has been that dyslexia does not exist: or if it does, it is incurable. Neurologists, most of whom would probably agree in believing that there is such an entity as dyslexia, certainly do not support any attitude of educational nihilism. On the contrary, in the recent renewal of interest in this problem, neurologists have been in the forefront in urging an official recognition of dyslexia, and in pleading for skilled screening of the cases, and for appropriate intense and sympathetic tuition of the victims at the hands of specially trained experts.

The lack of serious effort to assist these cases has led to an understandable demand upon the part of parents that some positive action is overdue and that delay can no longer be tolerated. As has happened before, the stimulus for research and treatment in a baffling medical condition has come from interested lay enterprise. Philanthropic organisations like the Orton Society, and the Invalid Children's Aid Association are now intervening in a commendable fashion, and offer a hopeful prospect for the future.

It is for reasons such as these that the subject of developmental dyslexia is topical and even pressing. Consequently it was considered appropriate to expand the Doyne Memorial Lecture for 1961 upon the subject of "Inborn Reading Disorders of Central Origin," so as to constitute the scaffolding of this present monograph.

The chapters which follow seek to trace the growth of our knowledge of this condition, and to describe the conflicting ideas as to nature and causation. Just how these dyslexic children should be taught is an important question which has been deliberately avoided, for this is a technical problem in educational science which lies outside the competency of a neurologist.

A fairly comprehensive bibliography has been prepared, in the belief that even if neurological hypotheses should prove unacceptable to the reader, a ready assistance with the literature might be rewarding.

The author would particularly like to acknowledge the co-operation which he has received in Copenhagen from Doctor Knud Hermann at the Wordblind Institute, and for acquainting him with the problem of dyslexia in Denmark both today and in the historical past.

Lastly, through the kindness of the Editor of the *Evening News*, I am permitted to make a verbatim quotation of a piece of anonymous fine writing which appeared in a leading article on August 9th, 1926:

The Case of the Unlettered

" 'Although sharp at all other things,' the boy could not read. He was thirteen years old: at thirteen years a boy's reading lessons should be over and done. Yet he could not read: or, if he might read at all, it was only such words as 'cat' and 'rat'.

"Therefore he died, which seems heavy punishment for being dull at his reading. The tramway which runs on Southend Pier is an electric tramway. It is fenced about with railings. What are railings that they should keep a boy from climbing over them? But, besides the railings, there were placards warning all who should approach of the dangers of the live rail.

"If the boy could have read the placards he would not have climbed the railing. But the placards told him nothing, he being able to spell out only the simplest words. So he climbed and took his death from the current.

"The world is like that, a perilous world for those who cannot learn to read. It must be so. We cannot fence every peril so that the unlettered may take no harm from it. There is free and compulsory education: at least everybody has his chance of learning his lessons in school. The world's business is ordered on the understanding that everybody can at least spell out words.

"We walk in obedience to the written word. All about us are boards and placards, telling us to do this thing or to keep from doing that other thing. Keep to the Right, we are bidden, or else we are to Keep to the Left. By this stairway we are to descend to enter the train that goes Westward: by that we go to the Eastward train. Way Out and Way in; Private; Trespassers will be Prosecuted; Pit Entrance; the street's name and the name of the railway station—all of these things are cried out to us by that wonderful device of letters, a babble of voices which make no sound.

"It is hard for us to understand the case of those to whom these many signs and warnings say nothing. They must move as though bewildered, as though they were blind and deaf. No warning touches them, not even that of the board which, like the board of the Southend tramway, cries Danger and Beware.

"Yet they go about their business in that darkness, in that silence. In some fashion they move, keeping shyly beside us lettered folk. Last month one of them sat near to me in a carriage of the underground railway. He asked me how many stations lay between us and the Monument station. I told him that we were not yet near the Monument, but that he was in the right train. But this was not enough: he must needs tell me that he could not read so much as a station's name.

"He seemed a man of sound wits. I dare say that, like the boy killed on Southend pier, this man was 'sharp at all other things'. He wore a coat as good as mine and had the air of one who prospered in the world. But when he told me suddenly that he could not read, I was shocked to hear him: it was as though he had revealed some deformity to me. Indeed I should have looked less curiously at a legless man.

"There he was, in a town all noisy with letters and words, in a carriage full of men reading the news of the world in their newspaper, in a London full of printed stuff, of boards and placards each giving its tidings. Yet he was travelling like a blind man, asking his way, asking help as he went. Another must expound to him the meaning of the plates with the word *Monument* painted on them. Then he would get out of the train and look cunningly to see by which of the staircases men were mounting to the street, for the words Way Out tell him naught. In the course of the day he must have asked many questions and told many men that he could not read.

"When you consider what pains he would be at daily, it would seem easier for him to learn the art of reading than to ask so many questions. For by his speech I took him for a fellow Londoner. On the uplands a man may plough and sow, year in and year out, without ever troubling himself to know the word 'cat' from the word 'rat'. In London the unlettered man must live as one maimed and helpless. But I take it that this poor fellow was one of those whom no teacher might teach to read.

"Indeed I think that there are many such. There are degrees in their ignorance. The man in the train told me that he could read no word. The boy at Southend could read 'cat' and 'rat', although the warning words of the board could not warn him. There are others who can, by setting their wits at it, slowly spell out a sentence, although they do not put themselves willingly to such a task. But none of these can read as we read, to whom the print of whole sentences, of whole paragraphs, speaks at once as we glance at them.

"Nature may have given them good brains and clear wits. Your unlettered man need not be fool or idiot: it is enough to say that there is some blind spot within his head, some flaw that will ever keep him from reading and writing, from all things that go with reading and writing. Sometimes the labour of the teacher will teach him something of these matters. But he will surely lapse when the teacher shall have done with him; then he will read no more, forgetting all that ever he learned.

"For such as he is, the days of school-time must be long days and weary days. I will not say that all the time is mis-spent: life nowadays is safer for the boy who can read the warning board, although painfully. But the case of the boy who could read only 'cat' and 'rat', although he was 'sharp at other things', should have its lesson for those who are taken by the strong delusion that we may see a world of book-learned men and women if we will spend the money handsomely. For it is not so: there will always be those who cannot get beyond 'cat' and 'rat', even some who cannot get so far."

Chapter I
The aphasiological context

Historically speaking, the current neurological conception of a specific and constitutional type of difficulty in learning to interpret verbal symbols, took origin from an experience of acquired brain disease, out of a process of analogy. Almost as long as aphasia had become recognized, neurologists became aware that in some cases of speech-loss the patient, in conspicuous fashion might lose his capacity of attaching "meaning" to printed or written verbal symbols. This particular defect is ordinarily termed "alexia" or "dyslexia". The traditional definition proposed by Bateman in 1890 may be quoted: "a form of verbal amnesia in which the patient has lost the memory of the conventional meaning of graphic symbols".

The earliest evidences of the recognition of such a disability are not easy to trace. The mystical writings of St. Teresa of Jesus (1515–82) reveal that during her states of ecstasy, words and letters would lose their meaning. Johan Schmidt (1624–90) was, according to Benton, one of the first physicians clearly to describe the loss of an ability to read. The retrospective account written by Professor Lordat of Montpelier in 1834 after his recovery from a speech disorder in 1825 affords a vivid description of his failure to make sense out of printed symbols. "Whilst retaining the memory of the significance of words heard"—so he explained—"I had lost that of their visible signs. Syntax had disappeared along with words; the alphabet alone was left to me, but the function of the letters for the formation of words was a study yet to be made. When I wished to glance over the book which I was reading when my malady overcame me, I found it impossible to read the title. I shall not speak to you of my despair, you can imagine it. I had to spell out slowly most of the words, and I can tell you by the way how much I realized the absurdity of the spelling of our language. After several weeks of profound sadness and resignation, I discovered whilst looking from a distance at the back of one of the volumes in my library, that I was reading accurately the title *Hippocratis Opera*. This discovery caused me to shed tears of joy".

Other early records of aphasia in which the patient became unable to comprehend printed and written words, were those described by Forbes Winslow (1861); Falret (1864); Peter (1865); and Schmidt (1871). Broadbent (1872) described the case of a man who had been knocked down in the street and had been taken to the Casualty department of St. Mary's Hospital, London. The injured man could not express himself very well and pointing to some printed words on the wall, said "I can see them, but cannot understand". He had had a

1

slight stroke a year before, since when, although able to write, he could not make sense of printed or written words with the exception of his own surname. Though able to converse pretty well he could never recall the names of objects put before him. Shortly afterwards he died from another vascular accident. Autopsy revealed two lesions, the older one, regarded by Broadbent as being responsible for the unusual type of aphasia, being in the region of the left angular and supramarginal gyri.

Kussmaul (1877) is usually credited with being the first specifically to isolate an aphasic loss of the ability to read, and he proposed the term "word-blindness" or *caecitas verbalis*. In his own words, ". . . a complete text-blindness may exist, although the power of sight, the intellect, and the powers of speech are intact". He stressed, however, that word-blindness, like word-deafness, is seldom an isolated defect, being generally combined with other dysphasic derangements, such as loss of words of an amnestic nature, or with agraphia. Dejerine (1892) placed the responsible lesion in the medial and inferior portions of the left occipital lobe, but he also surmised that destruction of the fibres connecting the two occipital lobes was significant.

The word "dyslexia" was first suggested by Professor Berlin of Stuttgart in 1887 in his monograph *Eine besondere Art der Wortblindheit (Dyslexia)*.

As more and more clinical examples were reported, it was found that patients with alexia (or dyslexia) could roughly be divided into two main groups according to whether the ability to write was retained or lost. Some alexic patients were still able to write even though they could not read back what they had written, unless of course the subject-matter remained fresh in their memory. The comment was often made that they wrote as though their eyes were shut. By way of contrast, were those patients who found themselves at one and the same time alexic and agraphic. It became customary to regard the former as examples of "subcortical word-blindness" and the latter as cases of "cortical word-blindness". For years the propriety of this schematization remained unchallenged. In like manner the conventional belief in an all-or-nothing state of affairs in alexia was accepted blindly, while fragmentary, incomplete or inconsistent deficits in reading were glossed over.

Another kind of dichotomy also came about, which looked upon cases of alexia without agraphia as instances of "agnosic alexia", in contrast to the cases of alexia combined with agraphia which were deemed to be examples of "aphasic alexia".

Finally there grew up a tendency to speak of cases of "pure" alexia (or word-blindness), implying thereby two conceptions both of dubious validity. In the first place lies the implication—rather than the explicit statement—that the inability to read is total. Secondly there is entailed the idea that the defect exists in isolated form, without any other disturbance of language. Modern aphasiologists, however, are critical on both scores, and suspect that in the allegedly "pure" cases of alexia, other disorders within the realm of language can always be uncovered, if only the investigator probes deeply enough. Contemporary students of aphasia look askance, furthermore, at any idea of totality within alexia. An absolute, complete and utter failure to interpret each and every verbal symbol is rarely, if ever, found as an acquired deficit.

Hence it is more correct to regard alexia as that variant of aphasia where the most conspicuous feature consists in an extreme difficulty in the interpretation of verbal or literal symbols by way of visual channels. This last point needs to be emphasized, for it sometimes happens that an alexic patient, unable to interpret at sight a letter or word, can deduce its meaning by dint of tracing the outlines of the symbol with a finger-tip, or by a deliberate sweep of the gaze over the contours. This adventitious technique of interpretation is often spoken of as "Westphal's manoeuvre".

In those rare cases of what is traditionally called "visual object agnosia" the patient finds great difficulty in identifying surrounding objects by way of sight. The perplexity also applies to persons and especially their faces; to pictures and illustrations; and of course to verbal and other graphic symbols. When some restitution of function begins to take place, the patient may more or less regain the power of recognizing objects; or perhaps some single item out of a medley of surrounding articles. Thus it comes about that three-dimensional data are distinguished at a stage when their two-dimensional representations are still elusive. Later still pictorial stimuli may be grasped, but comprehension of the meaning of letters and words remains imperfect. This, then, is an asymbolia—an alexia occurring as the residual disability in a case of agnosia. Other "parietal" defects also may be revealed by appropriate tests, such as constructional apraxia, the so-called "Gerstmann syndrome", spatial disorientation, defective recognition and naming of colours, or even a frank homonymous hemianopia. Pötzl asserted that alexia and "colour-agnosia" always occur together; although that statement goes too far, an association of these two conditions has certainly been commonly described.

Complicated errors of visual perception may sometimes be demonstrated in patients with this "agnosic" type of alexia. Thus a patient may assert that the printed matter he is looking at is blurred; or that the symbols merge one into another. Sometimes the patient's halting attempts at making out words or letters are assisted to some extent by he use of a magnifying lens. In other words an element of metamorphopsia of central origin may occur in some of these patients and this can perhaps account in part for the alexia, or at least it can aggravate it.

When discussing alexia, a distinction must also be made between the ability to read aloud with understanding of the text, and the power of silent comprehension. Ordinarily both performances are impaired in alexic patients, but occasionally some measure of dissociation occurs. Thus some patients can more or less grasp the significance of verbal symbols which they gaze at in silence; but when they read aloud, the meaning eludes them, although the pronunciation of the component words in the text may be accurate. In others it seems as though the double task of reading aloud and of comprehending is beyond the patient's competency. To this particular phenomenon Joffroy proposed the term "psycholexia".

To extract the meaningful content out of a printed or written text is a problem which varies according to the innate obscurity of the subject matter. This statement holds true independently of cerebral pathology. Thus, confronted with a text sufficiently recondite or elusive, every normal subject is a potential alexic. Three examples may be given, as tests of verbal comprehension:

(a) "Once upon a time there was a fat little pussy named Tommy who lived with his Mummy and Daddy in a pretty little house. Now although Tommy was a nice kitten to look at, I'm afraid he was the very naughtiest of all the kittens in the village".

(b) "The category of duration is called aspect. Our tenses express the moment in which an action is accomplished, is being accomplished, or will be accomplished. They take no account of the duration of such accomplishment".

(c) "A grief ago she who was who I hold the fats and flower, or, water-lammed, from the scythe-sided thorn, hell wind and sea, a stem cementing, wrestled up the tower, rose main and male, or, masted venus, through the paddler's bowl sailed up the sun".

Many ordinary readers will find (a) simple; (b) difficult; and (c) incomprehensible.

Of a rather special type is the case quoted by Bastian* where a printed text on being read aloud became a meaningless jargon, capable none the less of being articulated. This same passage has been incorporated by Aldous Huxley within one of his writings, not without certain light-hearted embellishments which certainly do not detract

---

*This case-report can be found in Bastian's monograph, "A treatise on Aphasia and other speech disorders", 1898, and refers to case 71, originally described by Dr. Osborne of Dublin. According to Bastian the patient read silently with full understanding, but emitted gibberish as he read aloud. The same case was also quoted by F. Bateman in the 2nd edition of his work on aphasia (1890).

An even earlier description of a grotesque distortion of a printed text when read aloud by an aphasiac was given by W. Broadbent in *Brain*, 1878–79.

from the narrative, though they do not add to its scientific import. This is how Huxley retailed it:

"Philip was dining alone. In front of his plate half a bottle of claret and the water jug propped up an open volume. He read between the mouthfuls, as he masticated. The book was Bastian's *On the Brain*. Not very up-to-date, perhaps, but the best he could find in his father's library to keep him amused in the train. Half-way through the fish, he came upon the case of the Irish gentleman who had suffered from paraphasia, and was so much struck by it that he pushed aside his plate and, taking out his pocket book, made a note of it at once. The physician had asked the patient to read aloud a paragraph from the statutes of Trinity College, Dublin. 'It shall be in the power of the College to examine or not every Licentiate, previous to his admission to a Fellowship, as they shall think fit.' What the patient actually read was: 'An the bee-what in the tee-mother of the biothodoodoo, to majoram or that emidrate, eni eni Krastrei, mestreit to ketra lotombreidei, to ra from treido as that kekritest'. Marvellous! Philip said to himself as he copied down the last word. What style! What majestic beauty! The richness and sonority of the opening phrase! 'An the bee-what in the tee-mother of the biothodoodoo'. He repeated it to himself. 'I shall print it on the title page of my next novel,' he wrote in his notebook. 'The epigraph, the text of the whole sermon'. Shakespeare only talked about tales told by an idiot. But here was the idiot actually speaking . . . Shakespeareanly, what was more. 'The final word about life', he added in pencil''.

Chapter II

Historical

Such was the background upon which the conception arose of a defect in the art of reading, which is inherent or inborn, and not brought about through disease.

In December 1895 and also in November 1896, James Hinshelwood, a Glasgow eye surgeon, wrote to the *Lancet* upon the topic of visual memory and word-blindness. The former publication prompted Dr. Pringle Morgan, a general practitioner in the seaside town of Seaford, where many preparatory schools are located, to describe a paradoxical case which he had seen, of an intelligent boy of 14 who was incapable of learning to read. This was one of the earliest and possibly the very first case subsequently to become known as an instance of "congenital word-blindness". In his original report in the *British Medical Journal* of November 7th, 1896, the author said "the school-master who taught him for some years says that he would be the smartest lad in school if instruction were entirely oral". Pringle Morgan sent Hinshelwood a reprint, and in a covering letter wrote: "It was your paper—may I call it your classical paper?—on word-blindness and visual memory published in the *Lancet* on 21st December, 1895, which first drew my attention to this subject, and my reason for publishing this case was that there was no reference anywhere, so far as I knew, to the possibility of this condition being congenital".

Actually Pringle Morgan had overlooked a note made a few weeks previously by James Kerr, Medical Officer of Health to the City of Bradford, and a pioneer school doctor. In 1896 Kerr was awarded the Howard Medal by the Royal Statistical Society for his essay on "School hygiene, in its mental, moral and physical aspects". Herein we find the following note . . . "But besides the generally dull there are the mentally exceptional, many quite suitable for ordinary school provided the teacher knows their peculiarities. Almost unique cases are found with most *bizarre* defects. Agraphia, for instance, may be unintelligible to a teacher, especially if it occurs, as in one of my cases, in a boy who can do arithmetic well so long as it involves Arabic numerals only, but writes gibberish in a neat hand for dictation exercise. *A boy with word-blindness who can spell the separate letters, is a trouble . . .*" (Italics not in the original).

Both Berkhan (1885) and Wilbur (1867) have occasionally been cited as pioneers in the history of developmental dyslexia. This is unlikely, for their patients were essentially mental defectives, and an inability to read was merely one aspect of their global defect in learning.

The initiative in the early detection of these cases remained for a time with British observers and especially with ophthalmologists. Among those who became interested were Nettleship, Thomas, Herbert Fisher, Treacher Collins, Sydney Stephenson, and Robert Walter Doyne. As if piqued by eluding the prize for priority Hinshelwood contributed a series of case-reports in the medical press between 1896 and 1902. In 1900 he issued his monograph upon "Letter, Word and Mind-Blindness".

Reporting two more instances in 1902, Hinshelwood wrote, "I have little doubt that these cases of congenital word-blindness are by no means so rare as the absence of recorded cases would lead us to infer. Their rarity is, I think, accounted for by the fact that when they do occur, they are not recognized. It is a matter of the highest importance to recognize the cause and the true nature of this difficulty in learning to read which is experienced by these children, otherwise they may be harshly treated as imbeciles or incorrigibles, and either neglected or punished for a defect for which they are in no wise responsible".

Outside of Great Britain the syndrome now became recognized and early reports came from Lechner in Holland (1903), Wernicke in Buenos Aires (1903) and Peters and by Foerster in Germany (1903; 1904). The first American observations were made by Jackson (1905) and by Schapringer (1906). Variot and Lecomte were the first to record cases in France (1906). By 1909, 41 cases had been reported in the literature (McCready).

What might be called the early history of this condition was closed by 1917, when Hinshelwood brought out his second monograph entitled "Congenital Word-Blindness". This period had been one of description and of identification. Thereafter began a stage of analysis and discussion with a considerable amount of change in orientation. It also ushered in an era of doubts, indecision, and confusion.

For various reasons, the bulk of research largely passed from Great Britain to the U.S.A., and even more so to the Scandinavian countries. However, within the past few years, after a phase of relative neglect, there has been a sharp revival of interest within this country.

Scientific attitudes towards the problem of failure to learn to read have oscillated like a pendulum over the past 70 years. Following Hinshelwood, there grew up the conception of a specific type of inherent aphasia which was at first termed "congenital word-blindness". From the analogy of acquired cases of alexia, a congenital aplasia of one or both angular gyri was visualized, as for example by Fisher (1910). This idea, be it noted, was entirely speculative, no pathological evidence having ever been forthcoming either in its favour or in rebuttal. Indeed, those who imagined some structural brain-defect began to find themselves in a minority, and to be outnumbered by those like Apert (1924) and Pötzl (1924) who visualized a developmental delay of functional rather than anatomical nature. Thus there arose gradually the conception of a "maturational lag" to explain the dyslexia.

In 1925 Samuel T. Orton entered the scene. As Director of the Greene County Mental Clinic in Iowa he discovered among a series of retarded children no fewer than 15 who could not read. His first patient was a 16-year-old boy from a junior high school, who had never been able to read. As the boy himself told Dr. Orton: "Mother says there is something funny about me, because you could read anything to me and I'd get it right away, but if I read it myself, I couldn't get it". Orton's interest was aroused, and he visited England in order to put the problem before Henry Head, then in retirement. From close observation of these retarded readers, and from a study of their imperfect efforts at writing and spelling, Orton found other important phenomena. There appeared to exist noteworthy correlations, such as left-handedness or ambidexterity, and a tendency towards reversals when attempting to read and to write, sometimes culminating in frank mirror-reading or mirror-writing. Orton believed that behind all these phenomena lay a basic state of ambiguous occipital dominance, physiological in nature representing a faulty patterning of brain function. For this condition which constituted a kind of graded series, Orton proposed the term "strephosymbolia".

Although this expression has never really gained acceptance, Orton's work broke new ground and directed attention to factors which we now believe may be important in the understanding of delayed ability to read. In his Salmon Lectures for 1936 (which were not published until 1938) a summing-up appeared which has since been referred to as "The Orton Credo". "The view presented here that many of the delays and defects in development of the language function may arise from a deviation in the process of establishing unilateral brain superiority in individual areas, while taking account of the hereditary facts, brings with it the conviction that such disorders should respond to specific training if we become sufficiently keen in our diagnosis and if we prove ourselves clever enough to devise the proper training methods to meet the needs of each particular case". In the U.S.A. the Orton Society continues to do valuable work in co-ordinating studies upon developmental defects of language and in organizing appropriate facilities for teaching such victims. Orton's widow and former pupil, and one-time President of this Society, propounded in 1957 what she called "The Orton Story". The nine characteristics of the strephosymbolia as listed by her, would almost entirely apply to the contemporary notion of developmental dyslexia as held by most neurologists.

Orton arranged for Miss Ann Gillingham, one of his assistants in psychology, to work out a technique of training strephosymbolic children, in conjunction with Professor Stillman. The Gillingham system is now in use in many centres in the United States.

But even before 1925, the conception of a congenital word-blindness had become qualified by opinions of quite a different sort. What had hitherto been a medical province or responsibility now became invaded by sociologists and educational psychologists. Belatedly, perhaps, they began to probe the broader and more complex question of general scholastic inadequacy. Lloyd H. Thomson in his monograph on "Reading Disability" (1966) has summarized these historical aspects with admirable clarity. He recalled Augusta Bronner's work published in 1917 on "The Psychology of Special Abilities and Disabilities". Analyzing the defects in 7 boys she stressed that the act of reading in the case of the normal subject must entail the synthesis of quite a number of faculties. These include perception and discrimination of forms and sounds; association of sounds with the visual appearance of letters; linkage of names with clusters of letters, and meanings with groups of words; memory, motor, visual, and auditory factors; and motor processes as subsumed under processes of inner speech and reading aloud. The following year, Leta Hollingworth wrote a paper on "The Psychology of special disability in Spelling", wherein she stated that specific instances constitute 20% or less of the total population of poor spellers. She favoured environmental and emotional problems rather than an innate lack of spelling endowment.

Similar reluctance to think in terms of a constitutional specific disability in the matter of reading now began to loom in the literature. The illiterate or barely literate population among youngsters gradually became looked upon either as one facet of general intellectual sub-normality ("the mildest grade of imbecility", as Rieger called it), or else as the product of adverse environmental circumstances. Delayed or diminished powers of learning to read were now regarded—not as a clear-cut entity—but as a non-specific resultant brought about by a diversity of factors. Backwardness in reading became envisaged more as a problem in sociology than a medical issue. The newer ideas, therefore, were to the effect that cases of inability to read constitute a spectrum, comprising the intelligent but disturbed child at the one extreme, and the dullard at the other, the common feature being failure to learn to read, write and spell. Such psychologists seem either to have overlooked medical views as to a specific reading-defect, or to have frankly rejected them, denying its very existence. Thus the detailed and erudite studies upon reading-retardation made by Burt, Schonell, Vernon and Monroe, among others, scarcely refer to the specific and organically determined defect in reading held by neurologists. The multifactorial notion reached its peak when Robinson (1946) listed some 12 causes or varieties of reading-failure.

Among the psychologists who have visualized a smooth transition within the childhood population from normal readers downwards to those with reading handicaps, may be mentioned Monroe and Backus (1937), Meyer, Nørgaard and Torpe (1943), as well as Robinson (1947), Tordrup (1953), and Gates (1955). Both Hermann and Larsen have independently criticized this conception, and by a close study of the curves which represent the distribution of intelligence levels of school-children have demonstrated a small hump in the region of I.Q. <45. This was first described by Jaederholm and has since been supported by Pearson, Fraser Roberts, Smith and Strömgren. This hump suggests something more than natural variation, and can fairly be ascribed to the influence of some pathological process. In the context of reading ability this hump is probably to be attributed to the presence of children with developmental dyslexia.

Neurologists, however—while not denying that many cases of failure to learn to read fall outside their conception of a specific defect—are sceptical about some of these criticisms. Certain educationalists have surely been both muddled and opinionated upon this problem; they have also erred by focussing more upon questions of aetiology rather than of cure. Neurologists too have been at fault, not so much in taking up too naïve a standpoint, as in being reluctant to challenge their critics and to press their views sufficiently. They have allowed psychologists to assert that neurologists regard dyslexics as incurable, and hence take a *non possumus* or nihilistic attitude. This is not really so. Neurologists believe that within the illiterate population there exists a hard core of specific cases which are neither psychologically determined nor yet an aspect of mental backwardness. The victims if recognized early and handled properly, can be rescued from the *limbo* of illiteracy, and by appropriate techniques can be taught to read with fair efficiency.

This brings us to the topic of the neurological conception and definition of developmental dyslexia. Here we may quote Hinshelwood's denomination put forward in 1917. "A congenital defect occurring in children with otherwise normal and undamaged brains, characterized by a disability in learning to read so great that it is manifestly due to a pathological condition and where attempts to teach the child by ordinary methods have completely failed". This is not wholly satisfying nor yet stylistically elegant. Skydsgaard's definition is crisper . . . "A primary constitutional reading disability which may occur electively". This viewpoint implies a defect in the visual interpretation of verbal symbols —an aphasia-like state: part of an inherent linguistic defect.

Schilder's definition (1944) stressed the mechanisms he deemed to be at fault "a primary disturbance of the sound-structure in the written words".

Eisenberg's definition is fuller. He would apply the term "specific dyslexia" to a situation in which a child remains unable to learn to read with proper facility despite normal intelligence, intact senses, proper instruction, and normal motivation. In this connection the term "specific" really implies an idiopathic condition, that is, one where the cause is unknown. Eisenberg's definition would be bettered if for "proper" instruction he substituted the adjective "conventional".

We may also recapitulate the definition advanced by Hermann: ". . . a defective capacity for acquiring, at the normal time, a proficiency in reading and writing corresponding to average performance; the deficiency is dependent upon constitutional factors (heredity), is often accompanied by difficulties with other symbols (numbers, musical notation, etc.), it exists in the absence of intellectual defect or defects of the sense-organs which might retard the normal accomplishment of these skills, and in the absence of past or present appreciable inhibitory influences in the internal and external environments."

Obviously it is no simple matter to formulate adequate definition and some authorities have abandoned all attempts so to do. The Research Group on Developmental Dyslexia of the World Federation of Neurology, which comprises an international body of experts—neurological, paediatric, psychological, pedagogic—met in 1968 and drew up two definitions which they recommended for general acceptance. These were as follows:

Specific Developmental Dyslexia

"A disorder manifested by difficulty in learning to read despite conventional instruction, adequate intelligence, and socio-cultural opportunity. It is dependent upon fundamental cognitive disabilities which are frequently of constitutional origin."

Dyslexia

"A disorder in children who, despite conventional classroom exper- ience, fail to attain the language skills of reading, writing and spelling commensurate with their intellectual abilities."

No neurologist would quarrel violently with Professor Burt when he wrote, "Many striking instances of so-called 'word-blind' children could be cited, who have made rapid and remarkable progress after a few weeks' intensive training at the hands of a psychological specialist" (1950). They would, however, quibble at the adjective "so-called", and they would scarcely imagine that adequate training would be a matter of "a few weeks".

The arguments in favour of the existence of a specific type of developmental dyslexia occurring in the midst of but nosologically apart from the *olla podrida* of bad readers, has been said to rest upon four premises. These comprise: persistence into adulthood; the peculiar and specific nature of the errors in reading and spelling; the familial incidence of the defect; and the greater incidence in the male sex. To these criteria may be added: the absence of signs of serious brain- damage or of perceptual defects; the absence of significant psycho- genesis; the continued failure to read despite conventional techniques of instruction; and the association of normal if not high intelligence.

Chapter III
Classification and terminology

By 1917 Hinshelwood was of the opinion that already both confusion in thought and loose terminology had developed. But he himself had contributed to the muddle when he proposed three terms: (1) "congenital dyslexia" for the commonly occurring, mildly backward readers; (2) "congenital alexia" for cases where inability to read was merely part of mental retardation; and (3) "congenital word-blindness" for the well-defined grave cases of pure reading defect.

These terms were unacceptable. Objection was also taken both to the adjective "congenital" as well as to the expression "word-blind". The latter had already been criticized as early as 1909. Alternative terms like "legasthenia", "word amblyopia"; "typholexia"; "amnesia visualis verbalis"; "analphabetia partialis"; "bradylexia"; "script-blindness"; "specific reading retardation"; and "specific reading disability" were put forward but never caught on. In the United States there was at one time a tendency to speak of "slow readers" as opposed to "retarded readers", the former being dullards, and the latter normal in intelligence. Yet other and less determinate expressions have been suggested, e.g. "psychic blindness", "symbolic confusion", "reduced reading disability", "developmental reading backwardness", "genetic dyslexia".

Rabinovitch (1954) isolated three groups of poor readers: (1) children of normal intellectual endowment who read badly because of various exogenous factors. Such cases he spoke of as examples of "secondary reading retardation". (2) (a) Children who were poor readers because of brain-damage; and (b) those endogenous cases without brain-damage, which he termed instances of "primary reading retardation". It was emphasized that cases of primary and secondary reading retardation differ in the degree of discrepancy between the items of the Wechsler scale intelligence test. Thus a considerable contrast (averaging 22·1) between the verbal and the performance intelligence quotients was claimed as characteristic of a primary reading retardation, while a lesser divergence (averaging 8·8) was believed to be suggestive of a secondary condition.

Among German authors, Walter (1954) favoured a non-committal term, namely *angeborene Schreib-lese-schwäche* (inborn defect in reading and writing). Nowadays however, the expression "dyslexia" is most popular, qualified by some such adjective as "constitutional" or "developmental". Who was the first to propose the Greek equivalent to the original term as used in the developmental connection, is not known. Most Scandinavian authors speak of "specific" dyslexia. For the less clear-cut cases where the dyslexia occurs alongside other disabilities—linguistic, neurological or psychiatric—some refer to "physiological variants of developmental dyslexia" or, simply, border-line cases. Where reading difficulties are closely associated with an underlying cerebral defect, the expression "symptomatic dyslexia" is appropriate. McGlannan (1968) used the term "complex dyslexia" in this connection. The distinction between "developmental dyslexia" and "dyslexia" *tout pur* as expressed in the definitions proposed by the World Federation of Neurology, turns upon the existence in the former of unequivocal genetical factors.

The outmoded term congenital word-blindness received a temporary fillip from Bosworth McReady (1926–7) who, while recognizing that other titles might be scientifically more exact, considered congenital word-blindness "a good robust sounding term, sanctioned by usage of earlier observers". He believed that it was the term which would most likely survive in a medical literature "already encumbered with verbal complexities". For different reasons it was the term preferred by various lay bodies, like the Invalid Children's Aid Association in Great Britain who have so successfully filled the gap in our educational system by providing skilled individual instruction to dyslexic children. In Denmark the title "Word-blind Institute" has been officially recognized. Nevertheless, congenital word-blindness must be looked upon as now obsolete as a scientific term, being largely replaced by the expression "developmental dyslexia".

A recent trend has been to avoid precision of thought and nomenclature by including the concept of dyslexia within a medley of other disorders. Thus "language disability", "learning disability", "perceptual disorders" are terms which have crept in, and have added confusion to the topic of developmental dyslexia. It would be better to avoid this kind of toponymy.

The three terms "specific dyslexia", "developmental dyslexia" and "specific developmental dyslexia" will be used interchangeably throughout this work.

Chapter IV
Linguistic and pedagogic considerations

The inherent complexities of a written language must not be forgotten. The conversion of a spoken language into graphic symbols is at the very least a two-fold problem, for the characters have to indicate not only the phonetic properties of the word, but also its meaning. In other words, the claims of both phonemics and morphemics must be satisfied.

If the neurological conception as to the constitutional nature of developmental dyslexia be the correct one, then considerations of a linguistic or educational character play a subordinate if not irrelevant part in the aetiology. Naturally these factors, if unpropitious, will still further handicap the dyslexic child who is struggling with the formidable task of coping with verbal symbols.

This "constitutional" view was not always held to be so. Claiborne long ago blamed dyslexia—or "word amblyopia" as he called it—upon the arbitrary pronunciation of the English language, and he seemed to doubt whether this disability ever occurred in those whose mother-tongue was Italian, Spanish or Russian. He was obviously not correct as experience has abundantly shown. None the less, the fact that English, like Chinese, and to a lesser extent French and Danish, is no logical orthographic language and is not necessarily spelt as it is pronounced, or pronounced as it is written, must erect certain barriers. It is not that dyslexia is unusually common in England, but rather that dyslexics are identified more readily and more early by dint of their failure to master our odd spelling. Like Stephenson, I have met more than one dyslexic schoolboy who found Latin easier than English. Though one might be tempted to ascribe this paradox to the more logical orthography of Latin, other factors may have been operative, such as for example the procedure whereby Latin had been taught.

It is now realized that developmental dyslexia certainly occurs in countries where the written language is more strictly phonetic, such as Germany, Spain and Latin America, Holland, Roumania, Czechoslovakia, Greece, and Italy. Unfortunately little is known about the incidence of dyslexia in countries where the written language differs fundamentally from the European patterns. There is good reason to believe that dyslexia also occurs in China and in India, but the exact pattern of the defect has yet to be identified. There have been a few case-reports from Japan, e.g. by Obi (1957), and by Arzai, Iwata and Ikeda (1966). Kuromaru and Okada (1961) referred to a 12-year-old dyslexic boy, who experienced more difficulty in reading the syllabaric Kana script than the ideographic Kanji symbols of Chinese origin. It

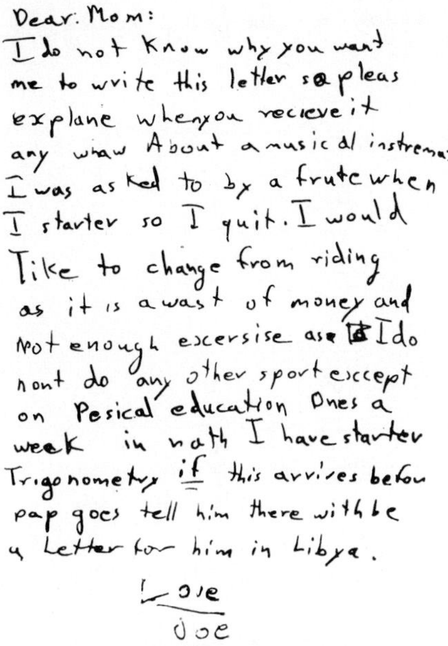

Dear: Mom:
I do not Know why you want
me to write this letter so pleas
explane when you recieve it
any whow About a musical instremet.
I was as ked to by a frute when
I starter so I quit. I would
like to change from riding
as it is a wast of money and
Not enough escersise ase I do
nont do any other sport except
on Pesical education Ones a
week in math I have starter
Trigonometry if this arrives befou
pap goes tell him there with be
u letter for him in Libya.

Loie
Joe

Dear Mom,

I do not know why you want
me to write this letter so please
explain when you receive it
any now. About a musical instrument
I was asked to buu a flute when
I started so I quit. I would
like to change from riding
as it is a waste of money and
not enough exercise as I do
not do any other sport except
on physical education once a
week. In maths I have started
trigonometry. *If* this arrives before
Pop goes tell him there will be
a letter for him in Libya.
Love,
Joe.

Fig. 1 Errors in spelling contained in a letter written by a dyslexic bilingual Anglo-Lebanese boy of 14 years and 6 months.
The boy's letter is on the left: the correct version is on the right.

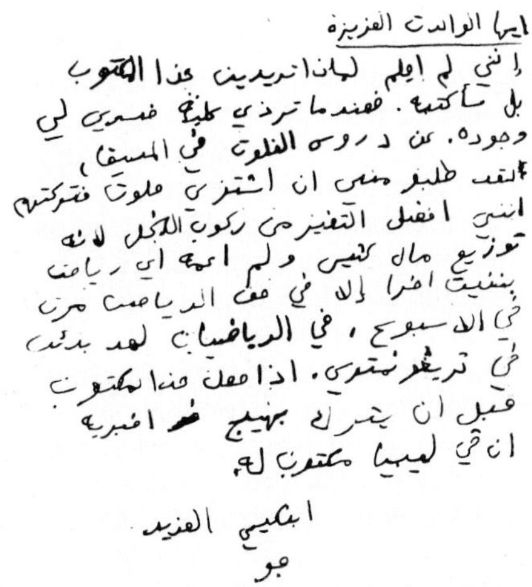

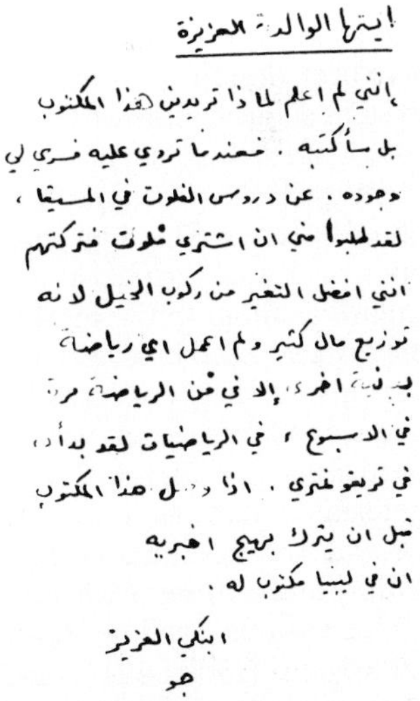

Fig. 2 The same letter, written in Arabic. Numerous errors are to be found by comparing the boy's version on the left, with the correct version on the right.

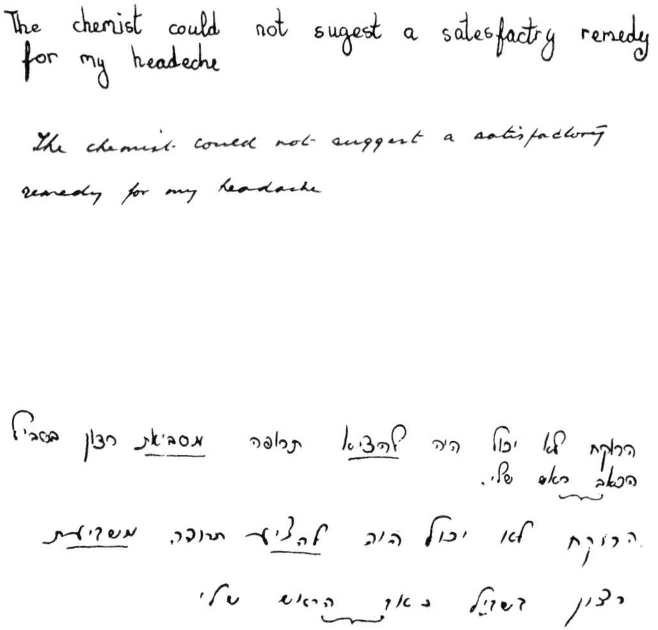

The chemist could not sugest a salesfactry remedy for my headeche

The chemist could not suggest a satisfactory remedy for my headache

Fig. 3 Inaccurate writing both in English and in Hebrew by a bilingual Anglo-Israeli dyslexic girl aged 14 years and 2 months. The first line in Hebrew is written by the patient, below which is the correct version. Her preferred direction of automatic gaze was from right to left. Crossed lateral, right-eyed. Reading age 10 years.

is interesting to recall that in those rare cases of acquired aphasia which have been described in the Japanese, the Kana script seems also to have presented more difficulty than the Kanji, and understandably so. In 1968 a surprising paper appeared from Tokyo, by Makita, who drew attention to the extreme rarity of reading disability among Japanese schoolchildren. This low incidence he ascribed to logicality of the two types of Kana scripts, as contrasted with the inherent difficulties of English orthography. In this way Makita harked back to the error first promulgated by Claiborne.

In my series there have been three instances of dyslexia in Anglo-Arabs, and errors in writing and spelling were detectable in both languages. (See Figs 1, 2 and 4.) There is good reason to believe that dyslexia is met with among schoolchildren in Jordan. I have also encountered a bilingual Israeli dyslexic with comparable defects in reading and writing. (See Fig. 3.)

The various spelling reforms which have come about in official Norwegian (1907, 1917, 1938) have been blamed as a disturbing influence upon dyslexics, greater than in other Scandinavian countries. Here again exact information is needed.

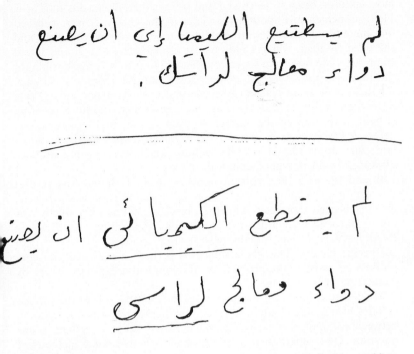

Fig. 4 Incorrect writing to dictation carried out by a bilingual Arabic speaking dyslexic boy of 13 years and 8 months. The upper specimen is written by the patient, and the lower is the correct version. The principal errors include rotations of individual symbols; reversals of groups of symbols; occasional wholly inaccurate symbols; and confusion of symbols which are similar in sound (TE and TA) although very different in appearance.

Of particular interest would be a comparative study of the incidence of dyslexia in Turkey, where after the revolution there was a compulsory replacement of the right-to-left Arabic script by a left-to-right European mode of writing. A similar problem is likely to arise in China if reformists succeed in their efforts to impose a Western typology.

One must also bear in mind the possibility that bilingualism, whether enforced or facultative, may lay an added burden upon poor readers, and so lead to a very early identification of cases of dyslexia. Of Chesni's series of Swiss dyslexics, 22·5% were obligatory bilinguals, coping with both French and German. This complicating factor of plurilingualism has been evident in several cases which I have observed.

The question arises whether the techniques adopted by those who teach children to read, play any part in either helping or handicapping dyslexics. There is still some doubt as to the optimum age at which a child should receive its first lessons in reading. In the United Kingdom

D.C.

most children begin to learn at 5 and serious reading-lessons start at 6. The age-incidence is about a year later in the U.S.A. Bender believed that there is a danger in starting children to learn to read too early, and she cited Sweden, where children first attend school at 7, and where some psychologists have suggested that the late start is responsible for the relatively low incidence of dyslexia. Even this premise is suspect, for there is no good reason to believe that dyslexia is particularly rare in Sweden. Views such as these are not convincing, and little attention is paid to the role of the mother in teaching the child its letters long before it first attends school. In any event an unduly early or unduly late start upon formal reading lessons could not possibly produce dyslexia, though it might facilitate diagnosis.

Bound up with the problem of when a child should first receive instruction in reading is the notion of "reading-readiness". Special tests have been fabricated with the object of determining whether or not a particular child is ripe for lessons in reading. A "Reading Readiness Chart" has actually been devised, made up of no less than 20 specific factors. The whole subject is perhaps a little artificial, and unlikely to assist in the problem of developmental dyslexia, except by facilitating early diagnosis.

Much discussion has also surrounded the possible role of the various systems of teaching children to read. Whether there exists a correlation between techniques of learning and eventual skill in spelling is one question. Quite apart there is the problem whether some methods of teaching children to read have led to a more ready recognition of dyslexics. Many have agreed with Walcutt in blaming dyslexia upon the various analytic, look-and-say, "flash" "see-and-say" global systems of teaching which concentrate upon the early identification of a word with its meaning, rather than its sound.* In 1960 the San Francisco Curriculum Survey Committee included among its recommendations, one which was headed ... "Reading: the Basic Importance of Phonics". While admitting the vagaries of the spelling of English, they considered the phonic system to be "rational enough" and felt that it encouraged children to think rather than to guess, and that its introduction would bring about a marked improvement in reading. Those who hold this view also believe that the synthetic techniques, whether phonic or syllabic (but not alphabetic), though out of keeping with *Gestalt* concepts of learning, possess certain merits where poor readers are concerned. A lighter burden is imposed upon dyslexics. It would be fair to say that no one particular method of teaching can *cause* a condition of dyslexia, but by dint of its combined merits and demerits, it may lead to an earlier recognition of word-

---

*Lloyd Thomson has reminded us that the phonic approach was coming under criticism as a learning technique over a hundred years ago. Pioneers in a whole-word method were Horace Mann (1838) and John R. Webb (1846).

blindness. Undoubtedly, sight-reading, as entailed in the analytic systems, presents special difficulties to dyslexics and also to "slow" readers of all types. When this global system was introduced into American schools in 1926, the progress in reading was assisted in the case of ordinary scholars, but the pupil who for one reason or other was unable to profit by this method soon became entangled in a web of confusion. Writing in 1937, Orton asserted that he had found three times as many reading-problems in children who had been taught by this look-and-say method. Monroe, too, preferred the old-fashioned phonic approach, saying darkly that it was better to be a slow reader than a non-reader.

Gray, whose primary interest was a crusade against world-wide illiteracy, found it impossible to determine on the evidence available just which was the optimum method of teaching. It may well differ according to the fundamental structure of the language concerned. We immediately recall that a phonic manner of learning written Chinese is virtually out of the question. According to Makita, Japanese school-children are required to learn the total 48 Hiragana symbols in their first grade, and the complete 48 Katakana symbols in their second grade. This type of learning is phonic. As regards the Kanji script, which has to be mastered in a look-say fashion, Makita asserted that the first grade scholar is expected to be familiar with 46 Kanji symbols, while in the 2nd, 3rd, 4th, 5th and 6th grades the scholar should have learned 105, 187, 205, 194 and 144 additional symbols. Dyslexia is betrayed in the Kana script in the first two grades of schooling, but throughout all the grades as far as the Kanji symbols are concerned.

There seems to be general agreement on one or two scores: (1) that a switch from synthetic to analytic systems of reading assists the quick reader; (2) that the flash method increases the incidence of poor spellers, even among adults; (3) that it also imposes a burden upon backward readers which many may never be able to surmount; and (4) that under a flash system of learning the true developmental dyslexic soon becomes conspicuous by reason of his shortcomings. This leads to readier discovery, with an apparent increase in the incidence of this condition.

A final implication, which will be considered later, is that a dyslexic, once diagnosed, should be taken away from a *milieu* where the analytic method of teaching is practised, in order to receive special instruction along totally different lines. At any rate this is probably desirable in so far as the English language is concerned.

The orthographic factor in dyslexia especially from the standpoint of early diagnosis would be an interesting project for research. There has been a serious endeavour within recent times to counteract the illogical spelling of the English language. This is exemplified in the Bernard Shaw extended alphabet, but even more so in Pitman's Augmented Roman

(A.R.) alphabet, also known as the "initial teaching alphabet" (i.t.a.). In the connection of developmental dyslexia, several questions arise: (*a*) Would the introduction of i.t.a. at the earliest stages of instruction in reading and writing lead to more, or fewer, instances of reading-retardation? (*b*) Can children later switch readily from i.t.a. to conventional techniques? (*c*) If so, what is the optimum age to make this change-over? (*d*) Does a preliminary learning-period with i.t.a. affect subsequent skills in reading or writing one way or the other? (*e*) Does a preliminary essay with i.t.a. constitute an additional burden to a true developmental dyslexic, thus leading to earlier diagnosis? (*f*) Or, does it on the other hand assist the developmental dyslexic, and thus postpone its eventual recognition? (*g*) Finally, does i.t.a. play any part in the treatment of a youngster or adult with developmental dyslexia?

None of these questions has yet been answered. The first two problems are under investigation at the University of London Institute of Education, while the last three topics have already been discussed and adopted as projects by the Research Group on Developmental Dyslexia and World Illiteracy of the World Federation of Neurology.

Chapter V
Maternal and socio-economic factors in aetiology

That birth-injury might constitute a factor in the genesis of dyslexia was first mooted by Fisher in 1910 at a meeting of the Ophthalmological Society of the United Kingdom. Various writers have since suggested that a trivial and unrecognized birth-injury may express itself in speech-retardation, and in later life by serious difficulties in learning to read. Thus Gesell in 1947 tended to associate reading disabilities with minimal birth-injuries. Warburg evoked a factor of maternal *Produktionserschöpfung* or weakness from excessive child-bearing or multiparity coupled with heavy manual work during pregnancy. Firm evidence, however, is not available, and it is indeed common to find dyslexia in first-born children, or in an only child of parents in comfortable social circumstances. The difficult question of birth-order and its possible significance in this connection, certainly merits specific attention. Harris (1961) stated that the "youngest or last-born boys were found almost twice as frequently in the group with learning problems". In my own series of children referred as suspected cases of dyslexia by reason of their difficulties with reading or with spelling, the birth-order was found to be probably non-significant (see Table). Premature infants have been said to develop a higher proportion of reading disabilities than full-term children. These statements are certainly not borne out in my experience, where neither large sibships have been conspicuous, nor evidence of perinatal damage, nor prematurity.

The most articulate exponents of a maternal aetiology have been Kawi and Pasamanick, who found that in 16·6% out of a series of 205 children with reading retardation, there had been gestational complications like pre-eclampsia, bleeding or hypertension. Of a control group of normal readers, maternal incidents of this kind occurred in only 1·5%. In these authors' view severe brain-damage leads to stillbirth, abortion and neo-natal death; while in a descending gradient, lesser traumata conduce to cerebral palsy, epilepsy, and behaviour disorders; whilst the most benign form of brain-damage is followed by faulty speech and congenital dyslexia.... "It would appear that a certain proportion of reading disorders might be added to the *continuum* of reproductive casualty".

Most neurologists, however, would be reluctant to visualize in developmental dyslexia any focal brain-lesion, dysplastic, traumatic or otherwise, despite the analogy of the acquired cases of alexia after cerebral-damage. To do so would be to ignore the important factor of immaturity as applied to chronological age, cortical development, and

processes of learning. In all probability the cases of reading retardation
which have been observed after brain-traumata at birth differ from the
genuine instances of developmental, i.e. specific, dyslexia. They probably belong to the category of "symptomatic dyslexias" where problems
in learning are associated with unmistakable and incontrovertible
evidence of cerebral damage. The confusion which pervades much of the
literature upon the subject of reading retardation and of "congenital
word-blindness" alike, is exemplified in this notion of antecedent
perinatal difficulties.

An interesting point is raised when the factor of adoption is considered. Although out of my total series of 620 cases of suspected
dyslexia I found in the family records a number of children who had
been adopted, there were no such instances in my random sample of
125 patients of both sexes. The generally accepted incidence in Great
Britain for adopted children is one in 41.

Socio-economic roles have often been mooted as possibly being
significant in the aetiology of "congenital word-blindness" as in other
learning-problems in children. Harris (1961) for instance, dealing with
the "language-blocked" child of average intellectual endowment,
found more boys from lower middle-class or lower-class families in the
non-learner group, where such factors as an inferior intellectual level,
want of motivation, lack of stimulation, and parental indifference as
to the boys' scholastic attainments seemed to exist. Comparable
remarks were also made by Mussen (1965) who asserted, but without
giving statistical support, that working-class children even a few months
old show a lower level of speech development than children of middle-
and upper-class parents. The factor of reading readiness, he said, is
also very much influenced by factors such as social class and verbal
stimulation in the home. Children from lower socio-economic groups
tended to score less well than those of the upper classes in tests for
reading readiness. Lower class children showed less evidence of
"achievement orientation" as he called it, than those from the middle
classes. In his survey (1968) of the children in the Isle of Wight aged
9 and 10 years, Rutter found 86 with "specific reading retardation".
This disorder, which may or may not correspond exactly with developmental dyslexia, was commoner in children with a working class
background, and it was twice as frequent in children from very large
families, i.e. 4 or more siblings. Perhaps these alleged factors of social
deprivation have less meaning in countries like Great Britain and the
Scandinavian group than in the United States. That early acquisition of
mature articulate speech can be fostered by a favourable environment
where the child is continually talked to and read to, can scarcely be
doubted. But this factor is unlikely to have any important bearing
upon the incidence of specific developmental dyslexia, whatever its
influence may be upon so-called reading readiness.

In taking a clinical history of patients with developmental dyslexia it is commonly found that the developmental milestones were attained and passed at a normal age. Miles, however, was impressed with the frequency with which infants, destined to become dyslexic, skipped the stage of crawling. We have no figures available from a control series, but out of my 125 cases referred to me as possible cases of dyslexia, 21 had never crawled.

The attainment of articulate speech is a matter which stands outside the other developmental stages, and will be discussed later.

Chapter VI
Clinical manifestations

"I struggled through the alphabet as if it had been a bramble-bush, getting considerably worried and scratched by every letter. After that, I fell among thieves, the nine figures, who seemed every evening to do something new to disguise themselves and baffle recognition. But, at last, I began, in a purblind groping way, to read, write, and cipher on the very smallest scale.

"One night, I was sitting in the chimney-corner with my slate, expending great efforts on the production of a letter to Joe . . . with an alphabet on the hearth at my feet for reference, I contrived in an hour or two to print and smear this epistle:
"mI deEr JO i opE U r krWitE wEll i opE i shAl soN B haBelL 4 2 teeDge U JO aN theN wE shOrl b sO glOdd aN wEn i M preNgt D 2 u JO woT larx an blEVE ME inF xn PiP."

Charles Dickens *Great Expectations.*

Before a description is given of the clinical characteristics of developmental dyslexia, the neurological attitude may well be once again stated clearly. Within the heterogenous community of poor readers (slow readers, retarded readers) there exists a syndrome comprising a specific difficulty in learning the conventional meaning of verbal symbols, and also in correlating sound with symbol in appropriate fashion. Such cases are earmarked, it has been said, by their gravity and their purity, a phrase which has become a cliché, not to be taken too literally. They are deemed "grave" in that the difficulty transcends a mere backwardness in reading, and the prognosis is more serious unless some special steps are taken in educational remediation. They are said to be "pure" in that the victims are free from mental defect, serious primary neurotic traits, and gross neurological deficits. This syndrome of developmental dyslexia is of constitutional and not of environmental origin, and it may well be genetically determined. It is unlikely to be the product of damage to the brain at birth, even of a minor degree. It is independent of the factor of intelligence, and consequently it may appear in children of normal I.Q., and it stands out conspicuously in those who are in the above-average brackets. Of course there is no reason why the syndrome should not at times happen to occur in children of subnormal mentality, when diagnosis might then be difficult. Other symbol-systems, e.g. mathematical or musical notations, may or may not be involved as well. This is an extremely interesting aspect of the problem which deserves special investigation. The syndrome occurs more often in boys. The difficulty in learning to read is not due to simple perceptual or acoustico-visual anomalies, but represents a higher level or cognitive defect—an asymbolia, in other words.

As an asymbolia, the problem lies in the "flash" or global identification of a word as a whole as a symbolic entity. Furthermore, the dyslexic experiences a difficulty, though of a lesser degree, in synthesizing the word itself out of its component units syllabic or literal. But the difficulties transcend a mere question of identification. There is actually a two-fold problem, comprising first that of interpreting the meaning of the word and, secondly, its appropriate sound.

The syndrome is often said to be "aphasic" in character in that it represents a *facet* of defective linguistic attainment. This is a precarious notion. It is unwise to seek too close an analogy between the non-appearance of a function and the loss of a function through disease. In any case, the term "aphasia" should not be applied to a failure in the development of a language-modality, but should be reserved for loss or impairment of a mature linguistic endowment.*

Having set out a descriptive account it would be useful to agree upon and adopt a definition of developmental dyslexia of workable brevity.

Some writers have attempted to draw up a sort of arithmetical or quantitative definition of dyslexia. Thus it has been looked upon as "a disability in which the reading-age lags behind the actual age by some 20% in spite of two or more years of regular attendance at school, with the usual exposure to both visual and phonic methods; a disability which does not depend upon emotional factors as far as can be judged. It carried additional connotations in that the disability is a familial trait, and furthermore it is related to mixed dominance".

In the foregoing definition we meet for the first time the term "reading age". This implies that something in the field of symbolic formulation and expression is possible on a par with the better known conceptions of "mental age" and "intelligence quotient". Attempts have been made to draw up a series of progressive verbal tests which children at different ages should read correctly. Sometimes the performance is correlated with school grade, as in the U.S.A., rather than with chronological age. One of the best known Reading Indices in the U.K. is that which is based upon the graduated vocabularies drawn up by Schonell.

Here we may re-assert the 1968 definition proposed by the Research Group on Developmental Dyslexia of the World Federation of Neurology.

---

*No satisfactory term exists to represent a failure of development of language in the growing child. "Alogia" would perhaps be the best pragmatic expression for the idea which is in mind, even though it has occasionally been employed in some countries in quite another context.

Definition

Specific Developmental Dyslexia

A disorder manifested by difficulty in learning to read despite conventional instruction, adequate intelligence, and socio-cultural opportunity. It is dependent upon fundamental cognitive disabilities which are frequently of constitutional origin.

Dyslexia

A disorder in children who, despite conventional classroom experience, fail to attain the language skills of reading, writing and spelling commensurate with their intellectual abilities.

From a study of the literature, as well as from the experience of interviewing children who are slow in learning to read, it becomes obvious that we require certain standards of reading texts to indicate the hiatus between the child's dyslexia and his chronological and mental ages. Too many tests are available, rather than too few, and many of them are based upon the American system of school grades and scarcely apply to children elsewhere. At the same time, outside the English-speaking countries, there are currently too few statistically established reading scales, and it is difficult to compare the degree of backwardness in reading between children belonging to different linguistic groups.

Among the techniques which have been favoured by Schiffman are the *Word Recognition Test* and the *Informal Reading Inventory*. These tests are duplex in character, for they comprise a flash approach which measures the sight vocabulary, and an untimed sub-test which demonstrates how well the pupil can emply "word-attack" skills. These are yardsticks of correct pronunciation rather than comprehension.

Monroe (1933) devised an elaborate index of reading ability depending upon the way a child fared with a battery of diverse reading tests. This author utilized a series of six basic investigations, viz.:

(1) *Gray's test*, where the child was required to read aloud paragraphs of increasing difficulty. Note is made of the time taken to complete the task, and also of the total number of errors. The results are transmuted into a score based upon the child's scholastic grade, which would range from one to eight.

(2) The *Haggerty Reading Examination*, (sigma 1, Test 2), a multiple choice test which measures the ability to read silently. Within a given time-limit, the child is required to underline the appropriate answers to questions of increasing difficulty. The score is made up of the number of correct answers, minus the number of incorrect ones. This test is suitable for children between the first and fourth American school grades.

(3) The *Monroe silent reading examination*. Here a number of paragraphs are followed by a question, and by several suggested

words, of which it is necessary to underline the appropriate one. A time-limit is imposed. The score comprises the number of correct words selected. This list is suitable for children between the third and eighth grades.

(4) The *Iota word test*, which measures the power of reading isolated words correctly. This test is applicable to children between the first and fifth grades.

(5) The *word discrimination test*. The correct word must be selected from lists of alternatives.

(6) The *Stanford reading-achievement test*. This is used whenever the child's reading-score lies above the norms of any of the previous tests.

Using the foregoing battery, Monroe constructed a "reading index" which aimed at taking into account a comparison of the child's composite reading grade with the average chronological, mental and arithmetical grades.

Other manners of expressing the extent of difficulty in reading have been devised. Thus de Hirsch *et al* (1966) spoke of an "overall reading performance test" (O.R.P.) as obtained by combining the scores in the Gates advanced primary and Gray oral reading tests. Macmeeken's (1942) "Reading quotient" expressed the attainment in reading as a percentage of the norm for a particular mental age. Kline *et al* (1968) calculated a "dyslexia quotient" (D.Q.) by comparing a child's grade attainment with his grade equivalent as judged by the Iota test.

As a practical measure, it seems advisable to have at one's disposal at least two types of reading-tests. Initially, there is scope for a group- or screening-test. This would prove useful in the hands of school-teachers who might thus be enabled to identify the backward readers out of a large group of children of the same age. Such a test is the reading section of the California (or Stanford) Achievement Test. Backward readers, weeded out in this fashion, will require further testing of a more individual character by way of tests like those employed by Schiffman or Monroe. By such techniques, the suspected cases of dyslexia might be sifted from the heterogeneous community of retarded readers, and then ear-marked for special neurological and psychological investigation.

In Great Britain the Schonell and Holborn scales are commonly used for testing accuracy in reading aloud, the Neale test being employed to measure the degree of reading-comprehension.

Perhaps the time is ripe for looking afresh at some of the conventional tests of reading ability, to ensure that they are as valid today as they were when first they were introduced. This is an educational research-product which is worth while, especially if the results are correlated among the geographical components of the English-speaking world.

Whatever routine tests be adopted in testing for dyslexia, careful attention must be paid to the speed with which the child reads aloud. Furthermore, the nature and number of mistakes should be observed and recorded.

Regarding the factor of speed it may be said that the rate of reading is usually reduced in the case of dyslexics, whether they read silently or aloud. Unfortunately but little information is available as to the reading-rates of normal children confronted with standard tests. Claparède was so impressed by this factor in dyslexics that he suggested the nosological term "bradylexia".

Bachmann (1927) was particularly interested in this quality of slowness in reading. He instructed six dyslexic and six normal children to read aloud a series of twenty-nine longish words (i.e. words made up of at least eleven letters). When the reading-time was measured with a stop-watch it was found that a dyslexic performed from $1\frac{1}{2}$ to 6 times as slowly as in the case of normals. Thus a word like *Strassenbahn-haltestelle* (tram-stop) took a normal child 2–4 seconds to pronounce, while a dyslexic of the same age took 39 seconds. *Hitzferein* took 2–4 seconds for a normal, but 115 seconds for a dyslexic. Bachmann illustrated the steps taken by the dyslexics in trying to master long and difficult words. Thus, shown the word *Handarbeitslehrerin* an 11-year-old dyslexic child after

	20 seconds said	*Hander . . .*
	40	,,	,, *Handbar . . .*
	60	,,	,, *Handbarweisstellerin*
and	90	,,	,, *Handarbeitslehrerin.*

Another 11-year-old patient was shown the word *Blitzableiter*.

After	9 seconds she said				*Blitzalbeiter*
,,	15	,,	,,	,,	*Blitzahlbeiter*
,,	24	,,	,,	,,	*Blitzableiter.*

According to Gray, whose primary interest was in international problems of illiteracy rather than individual dyslexia, the reading rates of normal subjects is surprisingly high. Thus the speed of silent reading in the case of university undergraduates was 5·63 words per second, without undue hurry, but as much as 8·21 at their fastest. When reading aloud the rate ranged from 3·55 to 4·51 words per second. Gray also quoted figures for the reading of Chinese, which can be accomplished even faster because of the compactness of the idiograms. Vertically orientated Chinese writing could be read more quickly than horizontal, the rate of reading varying from 2·8 to 20·7 words per second.

It is necessary to point out, however, that not every dyslexic child is slow in his reading performance. Particularly does this hold true for the "convalescent" dyslexic, that is, one who is beginning to make progress. In such, the teenager or adolescent may be observed to skim the text too quickly during silent reading, and, when reading aloud, to show undue hurry, accuracy being marred by erroneous guess-work. However, the majority of dyslexics and ex-dyslexics err by reading aloud too slowly rather than too fast.

Various classified lists have been made of the errors which a dyslexic child makes when reading aloud. Some have been enumerated by Monroe, and some by Goldberg, though each employed rather different attitudes towards the data. There are still other types of mistakes. Among the principal faults may be mentioned:

1. An inability to pronounce an unfamiliar word with a tendency to guess wildly at its phonetic structure.

2. A failure to realize the differences between words which are somewhat similar in spelling or in sound, e.g. PUG—BUD; ON—NO.

3. A failure to detect the differences in the auditory properties of words or letters.

4. Difficulty in keeping track of the correct place while reading.

5. Perplexity in switching accurately from the right hand extremity of one line of print to the beginning of the next line on the left. Mosse and Daniels have described this disability as a "linear dyslexia".

6. Lip-movements and subdued vocalizing of sounds while attempting to read silently.

7. Failure to read with complete understanding (as checked by such tests as the Monroe silent reading examination).

8. Incorrect pronunciation of vowels, e.g. BAG for BIG.

9. Incorrect pronunciation of consonants, e.g. BOLD for BOLT.

10. Rotations of letters, which constitute a most important type of error, and may entail mirror-opposite letters (according to the typology employed) e.g. *did* and *bid*, or *dad* and *bab*. Or the whole word may be reversed, so that the child may read WAS instead of SAW. Or again, short sequences or words may be read in a wrong order, as in the case of "DID HE" for "HE DID".

11. Inappropriate phonemes may be interpolated, as when the child reads TRICK instead of TICK.

12. Phonemes may be dropped from out of a consonantal cluster. Thus the child may read TICK instead of TRICK. Or whole syllables may be omitted, as when the child reads WALK for WALKING.

13. An error of quite different type is seen whenever the child substitutes one word for another, e.g. WAS for LIVED; THE for AN; THIS for THAT; HERE for THERE; and HIS for

HER. The word may be one which is approximate in meaning, or one which is metonymous.

This last is a particularly interesting type of error and a common one, though rarely discussed. The nature of the fault suggests that in reading aloud, the reader has identified the sense or meaning of the term but has substituted an alternative. Sometimes it is almost a synonym, as for example "shiny" instead of "bright"; "kind" instead of "good". More often a term is employed which obviously bears some association of ideas. Neither the actual word nor its substitute need necessarily be "difficult", polysyllabic, or unfamiliar. This phenomenon of word-substitution during the act of reading is not peculiar to dyslexics, for it may at times apply to normal subjects.

14. Words may be repeated in a perseveratory fashion, e.g. THE CAT THE CAT.
15. Words, inappropriate or otherwise, may be added, e.g. "ONCE UPON A TIME THERE WAS" may be read instead of "ONCE THERE WAS".
16. One or more words may be omitted altogether, e.g. "A DOG", instead of "A FIERCE DOG".
17. An omission of a different sort is seen in the phenomenon described by Monroe as a "refusal". Thus the child, attempting to read "ONE OF THE MOST INTERESTING" may say "ONE OF THE MOST ————" and then stop short.
18. Faulty placement of stress in polysyllabic words is common in those dyslexics whose reading age is comparatively advanced. It may well show in such long and perhaps unfamiliar words as "MISCELLANEOUS", "INORDINATE", "AUTHOR-ITATIVE".

Errors of this last type suggest that the patient may have met the word at one time in the course of his silent reading, but that he is hazy as to both its significance and its correct pronunciation. In any event he cannot correlate the appearance of the word with its acoustic pattern.

In her study of children who could not read, Monroe enumerated ten types of error, viz.: faulty vowels or consonants; reversals; addition or omission of sounds; substitution; repetition; addition or omission of words; and refusals. Recording these by the signs V. C. R. A. O. S. Rp. Add. Om. Ra. and Tot. (for Total) Monroe constructed charts to indicate a "profile of errors" by dint of Z-scores. An example can be given from a young adult (age not stated) who appears to a neurologist very like a case of developmental dyslexia. It must be emphasized, however, that Monroe did not use—and apparently did not approve—the term "dyslexia" and she referred to this patient as "a case of severe reading difficulty in an adult of average intelligence".

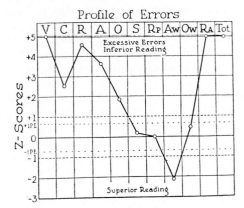

Fig. 5 Reading index 0·41 being case 27 in Monroe's "Children who cannot read".

The role of reversals in the attempts to read has often been played down by those who are sceptical as to the existence of dyslexia, asserting that many normal children perpetrate reversals at some time or other during their reading apprenticeship. But, as Money rightly asserted, the dyslexic individual is not unique in making reversals and trans-locations, but he is conspicuous in making so many of them and for so long a time.

When testing dyslexics as to their powers of silent or oral reading it is not infrequently found that the child performs no worse—sometimes indeed a little better—if the book is held upside down. This was so in Pflugfelder's patient, and it has been obvious in many dyslexics in my own series.

To some young dyslexics, letters standing in isolation possess little or no identity as units of a verbal sort, but instead they take on concrete non-linguistic properties. Thus to one patient, described by Faust, a capital X suggested a sawing-trestle, a capital Y was a pole support, an S was a traffic-sign, a capital P indicated police or else a post-office, a capital U was a rounded arc, a capital L . . ." something that had to do with police", and G was "an arc with a funny dash in it". Years before Dickens had referred to this same phenomenon of concretisa-tion when he wrote of Pip, in *Great Expectations*, identifying a large capital D with a design for a buckle. This is not the place to refer to psycho-analytical speculations about dyslexia, which are discussed later. It may be mentioned, however, that Klein (1949) went so far as to submit that the shape and appearance of letters (as well as their sound) often play an inhibitory role in reading, writing, and spelling, in that they may stimulate oral, anal, urinary or genital fantasies. Even earlier, Blanchard (1946) held the belief, and affirmed that a child, retarded in reading, may associate the letter C with a mouth open and ready to bite.*

Those interested in dyslexia can often learn much from an intelligent victim of older age whose defect in reading has become comparatively mild. The parents may proclaim with satisfaction that their youngster has at long last started to read for pleasure. They may go on to admit, however, that they are uncertain how accurately he interprets the reading matter. Their mental reservations are justified, for it is probable that the late reader, motivated by his interest in the subject-matter, does not allow unusual or obscure or polysyllabic terms to hold him up. He merely passes them by. Taxed upon this matter, the reader often has the insight and the honesty to admit the fact that he skips when reading.

Such a "convalescent" dyslexic will often assert that while now enjoying silent reading, he remains embarrassed when called upon to read aloud. He realizes that he does so slowly and haltingly; that he makes mistakes which may strike his audience as ludicrous or blame-worthy; and that in such circumstances he finds it particularly difficult to attend to the meaning. To ensure correct diction, while at the same time interpreting the text, is a two-fold and onerous task

An auditor with a keen ear may notice that the dyslexic, when reading aloud, lapses into certain dialectical or demotic methods of pronunciation which are absent from his conversational speech. In the case of a bilingual dyslexic, a foreign "accent" may become more evident when he reads aloud, although the converse might perhaps be expected.

The eventual reading-skill on the part of an "ex-dyslexic" may therefore be less efficient than would appear at first sight. Like so many other faculties which are acquired late, it is a vulnerable one, and the performance, whether at a silent or articulate level, is apt to deteriorate in circumstances of emotional stress.

The foregoing accounts of the difficulties in silent comprehension and in the articulation when reading aloud, will remind a neurologist of many considerations which are familiar to him from his experience of aphasic patients. He recalls that the very term "reading" is an

*A similar concretisation of units of the Greek alphabet was part of the romantic imagery of G. K. Chesterton. "To me," he wrote "the ancient capital letters of the Greek alphabet, the great Theta, a sphere barred across the middle like Saturn, or the great Upsilon, standing up like a tall curved chalice, have still a quite unaccount-able charm and mystery, as if they were the characters traced in wide welcome over Eden of the dawn. The ordinary small Greek letters, though I am now much more familiar with them, seem to me quite nasty little things like a swarm of gnats. As for Greek accents, I triumphantly succeeded, through a long series of school-terms, in avoiding learning them at all; and I never had a higher moment of gratification than when I afterwards discovered that the Greeks never learnt them either. . . . But it is a simple psychological fact that the sight of a Greek capital still fills me with happiness, the sight of a small letter with indifference tinged with dislike, and the accents with righteous indignation reaching the points of profanity."

imprecise one, for it entails a whole series of intellectual tasks which vary according to many circumstances, not the least of which is the inherent unfamiliarity of the subject matter. To begin with it is necessary to distinguish clearly between the problem of reading aloud and that of silent reading. These two activities are vulnerable in different degrees. As was specifically mentioned in the preliminary chapter dealing with aphasic dyslexia, a patient may be able to read aloud with fair phonetic accuracy but with limited comprehension. Or both comprehension and articulation may suffer. These observations hold true in the case of developmental dyslexia just as in aphasia.

As long ago as 1891 Freud emphasized the complexity of the ideas underlying the term "reading". The process of learning to read, he said, is very complicated and entails a frequent shift of the direction of the associations. There are several kinds of reading some of which proceed without understanding. A proof-reader pays special attention to the letters and other symbols, the meaning of which may escape him so that a second perusal is needed in order to correct the style. In an interesting novel, on the other hand, misprints are overlooked and it may happen that the reader fails to retain the names of the characters— except perhaps for some meaningless feature, or the recollection that they were long or short, or that they contained an unusual letter such as x or z. Again, during recitation, special attention is paid to the sound impressions of the words and the interval between them: the meaning may be overlooked especially if the reader be fatigued. These, according to Freud, are phenomena of divided attention which are of particular importance, because the understanding of what is read takes place over circuitous routes. Reading aloud is not to be regarded as a different function from reading to oneself, except that it tends to distract attention from the sensory part of the reading process.

The term "silent reading" is in itself, ambiguous. Some authors, e.g. Edfeldt (1959) seemed to equate silent reading with subvocal reading, i.e. the simultaneous utilization of silent movement of the lips and other articulatory muscles during the act of scanning a page of text. This is a practice adopted by inexperienced or retarded readers, especially if the text is a difficult one, or if the printed matter is blurred or unclear. This "silent", or better "subvocal", type of reading is probably habitual in cases of developmental dyslexia. Truly silent reading, that is without the intervention of whispers or movements of the lips or glottis, is the hallmark of the experienced and highly skilled reader who quickly scans a text wherein both vocabulary and subject-matter lie well within his intellectual capacity. This last point, namely that of competency, is important, for it suggests that there may be a level of task where even a normal adult is more or less temporarily dyslexic. Such a notion applies even more forcibly to an aphasic patient with an acquired lesion of the brain.

Yet another attitude towards the topic of reading and its deficits has been mentioned by Johnson (1961), who described three levels of attainment, namely: (1) a *functional* level where the child reads independently; (2) an *instructional* level where the child reads only in the classroom; and (3) a level of *frustration*, whereby the student misses half or more of the material that he is "reading". The author made the point that group tests of reading-efficiency measure only the frustrational level, while the various individual tests are capable of assessing all three levels.

Approaching the topic of reading from the standpoint of world literacy, Gray emphasized the graduated functional nature of the term. He distinguished an ascending order of interpretation of verbal symbols, viz.: (1) sign-reading; (2) the search for information and the satisfaction of curiosity; (3) the perusal of notices or directions; (4) the solution of problems; (5) thoughtful reaction; and (6) reading for pleasure. These scales are not inapplicable to dyslexics, who until they have mastered their particular disability, rarely admit to the practice of reading as a form of recreation.

A clinical point of importance—one with which every neurologist is familiar and psychologists sometimes overlook—concerns the characteristic variability of performance of the dyslexic child. The numerous faults in reading which have been enumerated may occur inconsistently in an individual case, being sometimes present but at other times not. The same applies to the written work. A dyslexic child may execute reversals, repetitions, omissions, intrusions and so on in profusion at one sitting but only occasionally at another. His alleged reading-index may vary from day to day, or from one hour of the day to another: he may fare better when reading subject-matter which interests him, than when the text is dull or boring (even though inherently no more difficult). Distractability, fatigue, and states of bodily health, are variable factors which should be given full attention.

Considerations of this kind convey a certain scepticism about the notion, so favoured by educational psychologists, of reading indices, reading age, educational profiles, and even of intelligence quotients. Schonell, for example, has spoken of a word recognition age; a comprehension age; a spelling age; multiplication ages; a mechanical age; a problem age; a composition age; and so on, in a manner which is alien to neurological thinking.

When applied to dyslexics, the "educational profiles" as drawn up for example by Monroe, give interesting data, which should, however, be accepted with caution tinged with a little scepticism. A typical example is given in the following charts, where three retarded readers (Monroe did not speak of "dyslexics") are recorded in respect of their performances. (Here O = Oral reading as measured by Gray's Oral Reading test; C = the comprehension of silent reading as determined by either the Haggerty or the Monroe scales; WA = word analysis, according to the Iota word test; and WD = word discrimination.)

Monroe's case 3 was a bright little girl of 7 years and 4 months with a mental age of 10 years, and an I.Q. of 135. She had a most engaging manner of distracting attention from her reading defect. "Let's don't do any reading. I know some arithmetic games that are lots of fun". Whenever a reading task was attempted she displayed considerable emotional tension.

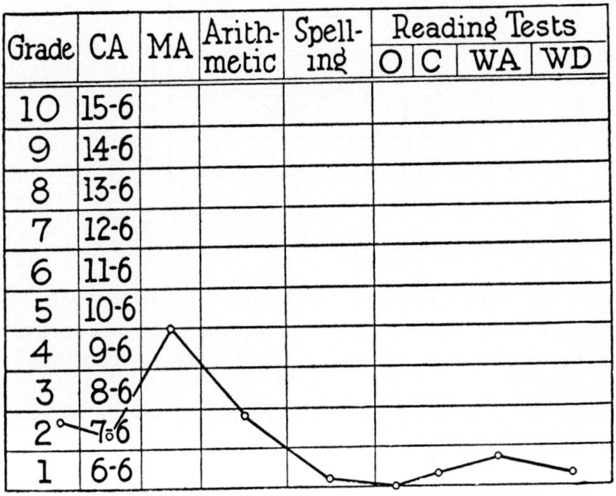

Grade	CA	MA	Arith-metic	Spell-ing	Reading Tests			
					O	C	WA	WD
10	15-6							
9	14-6							
8	13-6							
7	12-6							
6	11-6							
5	10-6							
4	9-6							
3	8-6							
2	7-6							
1	6-6							

Fig. 6 Educational profile of Monroe's case 3. Reading index 0·41.

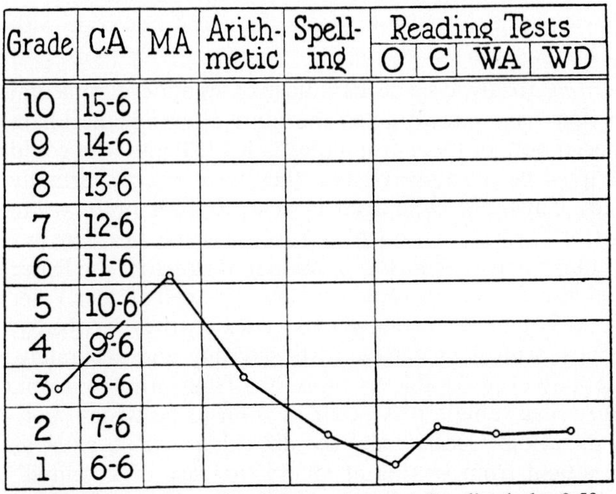

Grade	CA	MA	Arith-metic	Spell-ing	Reading Tests			
					O	C	WA	WD
10	15-6							
9	14-6							
8	13-6							
7	12-6							
6	11-6							
5	10-6							
4	9-6							
3	8-6							
2	7-6							
1	6-6							

Fig. 7 Educational profile of Monroe's case 4. Reading index 0·50.

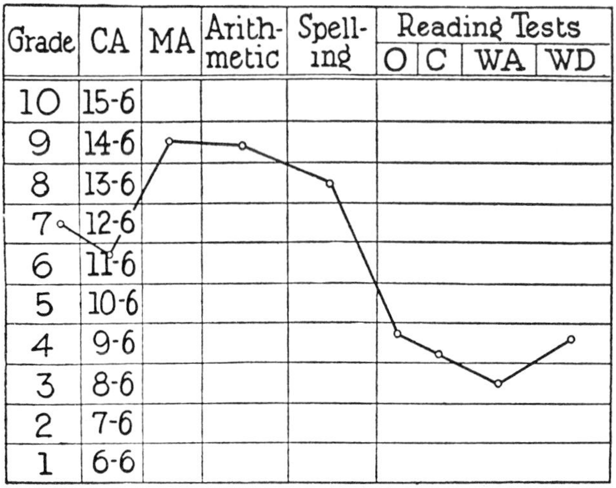

Grade	CA	MA	Arith-metic	Spell-ing	Reading Tests O	C	WA	WD
10	15-6							
9	14-6							
8	13-6							
7	12-6							
6	11-6							
5	10-6							
4	9-6							
3	8-6							
2	7-6							
1	6-6							

Fig. 8 Educational profile of Monroe's case 5. Reading index 0·52.

Her 4th case concerned a boy of 9 years and 10 months, with an I.Q. of 130 (on later testing 112). He excelled in mechanical activities. In his own words, "I wish I could learn to read, but I guess I'm too dumb".

Case 5 was a girl aged 11 years and 10 months, with a mental age of 14½ and an I.Q. of 122. Her arithmetical rating was at a superior level. The teachers commented upon her ambition, her social leadership and her general character, even though she admitted to copying other childrens' book-reports. She read so slowly and with so many mistakes that she could not cope with more than a few pages in an evening.

Disorders of writing are always considerable in cases of developmental dyslexia though they have not attracted the same attention. Berkham in 1885 made special note of these disabilities in his patients who could not read (but it must be remembered that they were almost certainly mentally retarded). Thus, one child aged 11 years and 2 months wrote *Der Ofen is Hor* (for "Der Ofen is hoch"). Another wrote *Der Shse mrt Slsl* (for "der Schlosser macht Schlussel"), *Die Rse st stre* (for "die Rosse sind Thiere"), and also *Der Vomten lont den Sonne* (instead of "der Vater lobt den Sohn"). Although every child who is dyslexic writes very badly, he can usually copy printed or cursive texts slavishly and accurately, albeit slowly. He may even be able to transcribe from print to script, or *vice versa*. But remarkable errors occur as soon as he writes spontaneously or to dictation. Occasionally the difficulties are so great as to preclude the patient from writing at all. In the case of a "cured" dyslexic, defective writing and spelling may continue to appear long

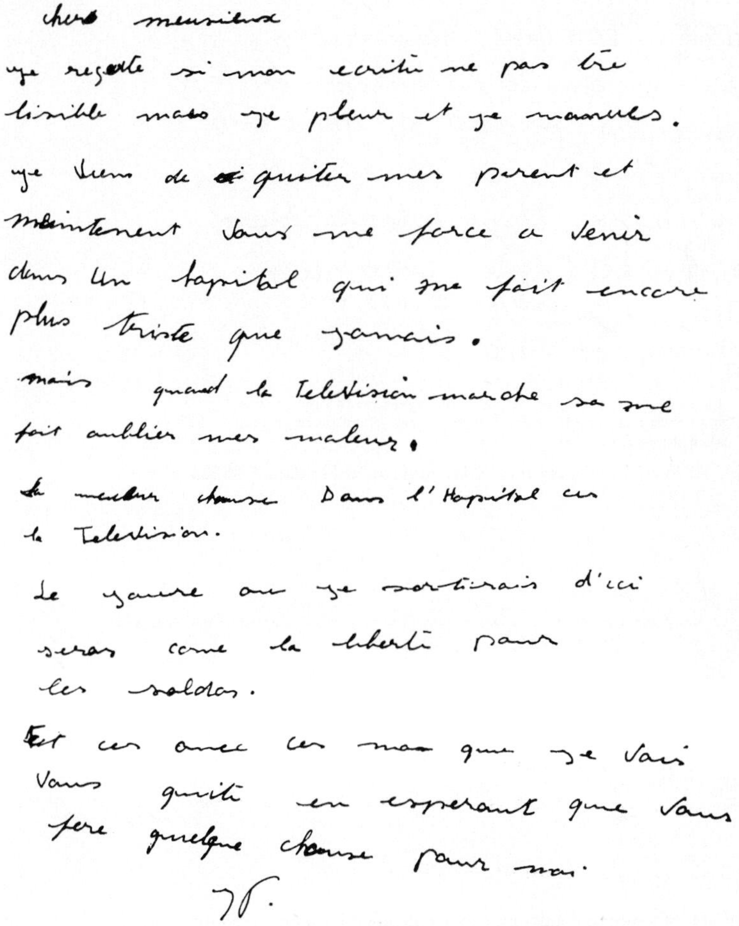
chers meusieux
ye regotte si mon ecriti ne pas tre
lisible mais ye pleur et ye manules.
ye viens de ~~ai~~ quiter mes parent et
maintenant vous me force a venir
dans un hopital qui me fait encore
plus triste que yamais.
mais quand la Television marche sa me
fait aublier mes maleur.
la meilleur chause Dans l'Hopital ces
la Television.
le yaure ou ye sortirais d'ici
seras come la liberti pour
les soldas.
Et ces avec ces mos que ye vais
Vous quiti en esperant que vous
fere quelque chause pour moi.
JB.

Fig. 9 Spontaneous writing executed by a French dyslexic boy, aged 15½ years.

into adult life. Where some degree of writing lies within the capacity of a dyslexic, the mistakes are of such a nature as often to make it possible to diagnose the reading defect from a mere perusal of the script.

In Great Britain we still rely upon the spelling scales for normal children as compiled by Schonell, or by Morrison and McCall. We need the assurance of educationalists that these standards are still operative, and not in need of critical re-examination.

Disordered handwriting associated with developmental dyslexia has been noted from the earliest days of this century, but the subject was first specifically and closely studied by Hermann and Voldby in 1946.

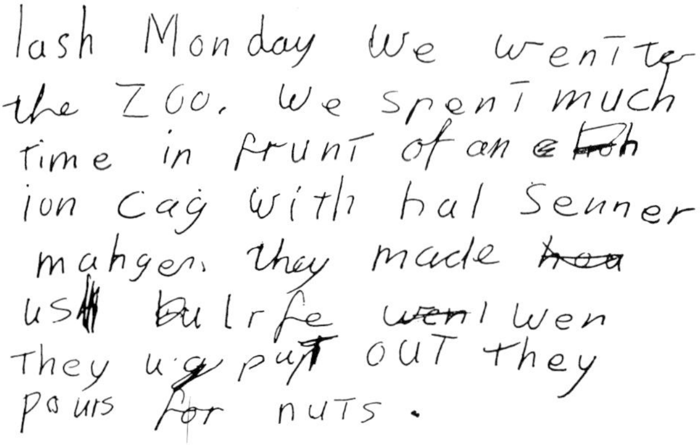

lash Monday We wenTTe
the Zoo. We spenT much
Time in frunT of an e froh
ion cag with hal Seuner
mahgen they made hrea
ush bul rfe wenl Wen
They ug puT ouT they
pa urs for nuTs .

Last Monday we went to the Zoo. We spent much time in front
of an iron cage which held seven monkeys. They made us laugh
when they put out their paws for nuts.

Fig. 10 Writing to dictation. R.G., male aged 11 years. C88584.

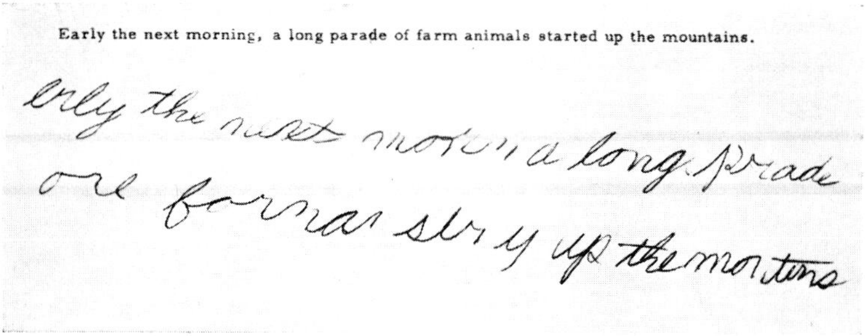

Early the next morning, a long parade of farm animals started up the mountains.

Fig. 11 Writing to dictation. R.S., male aged 13 years.

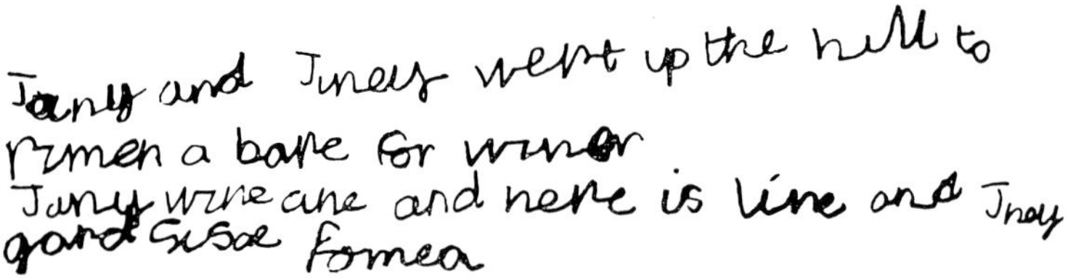

Jack and Jill went up the hill to fetch a pail of water
Jack fell down and broke his crown, and Jill came tumbling after.

Fig. 12 Writing to dictation. J.L., male aged 9 years. C85073.

it is ho   sdoe Mr lise aned to more
the   bdves a red and a

voen

It is hard said Mr. Lemon Hart to make the choice between
a red and a yellow rose.

Fig. 13 Writing to dictation. C.C., male aged 11 years. C89235.

Fig. 14 A fusion of the two consecutive letters "h" and "e" in the word "the". T.D., male aged 13 years. A5794.

Fig. 15 Fusion of letters; omission of letters; neographisms, illustrated in the word "School". K.H., male aged 12 years.

Fig. 16 "Arithmetic", written by M.M., female aged 16 years.

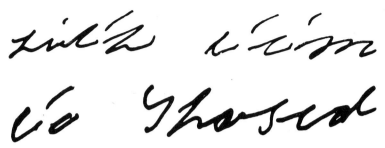

Fig. 17 "Lifetime", "two thousand", written by M.M., female, now aged 21 years.

Though their observations were made upon Danish children, their findings apply with equal force to English dyslexics.

An overall untidiness of the penmanship is common, but not essential, for very occasionally a dyslexic will write neatly with all the errors conspicuously displayed. However, untidy writing is the usual state of affairs. Some words are frankly illegible, while in others individual letters are often so malformed as to be barely recognizable. In this way some of the errors in spelling are concealed, and one is often tempted to consider this a deliberate manoeuvre. Among the characteristic defects in writing, the dyslexic may show: mal-alignment; intrusion of block capitals into the middle of a word; omissions or repetitions of words and letters; rotation of letters; odd punctuation marks; and mis-spellings. Besides the common errors of the ignorant speller, unusual and even extraordinary mistakes are to be found. One typical fault consists in the partial or complete reversal of groups of letters, so that for the word NOT we may find ONT or TNO, or even TON.

Just as in the case of reading, reversals of letter-groups are not rare in the earliest efforts at writing made by normal children. Here again dyslexics differ in showing more of these reversals and in continuing to perpetrate them for an inordinate length of time.

Noesgaard (1943) studied the characters of spelling mistakes in normal Danish schoolchildren. His case-material consisted of 300 children aged from 9 to 12, in the 3rd and 6th school years. Hermann compared the errors made by his dyslexics with Noesgaard's findings, as in the following table. (Table 1, p. 41.)

Quite apart from reversals, are the rotations of letters whereby the writer shows a frequent confusion of b with d; less often between h and y. A common characteristic, especially in block writing, is an incorrect positioning of certain letters, so that E appears as Ǝ, N as И, S as Ƨ. At times an actual fragment of mirror-writing is found, especially when the dyslexic holds the pencil in his left hand.

Another characteristic of the dyslexic's writing is an unorthodox manner of joining up adjacent letters. Thus the linkages may be either

TABLE I

Test Word	Noesgaard % age		Hermann % age	
	Total No. of errors	Total No. of reversals	Total No. of errors	Total No. of reversals
STRAKS (immediately)	11	2·2	99	10
MARTS (March)	21	11	78	26
SLAGS (sort) . .	24	1·2	81	9
FUGL (bird) . .	16	10	62	10
KORN (corn) .	3·3	0	37	3
ORM (worm) .	0·3	0	40	4
VOGN (vehicle) .	4·2	3·2	75	30

The greater incidence of reversals among the word-blind is obvious.

too long or too short; or the strokes may intersect (see illustrations). One letter may fuse with the next to form a strange merger, difficult to identify out of context. This kind of error is spoken of as a "contamination". Even more typical are the "neographisms", that is, literal symbols foreign to any accepted system of typology (see illustrations).

The spelling mistakes in the writings of dyslexics differ in many respects from the errors made by normal uneducated subjects or by

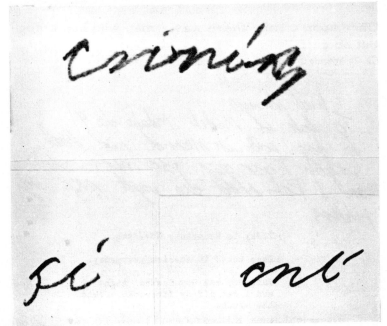

Fig. 18 "Crying", "if", "not", written by M.M., female, now aged 21 years.

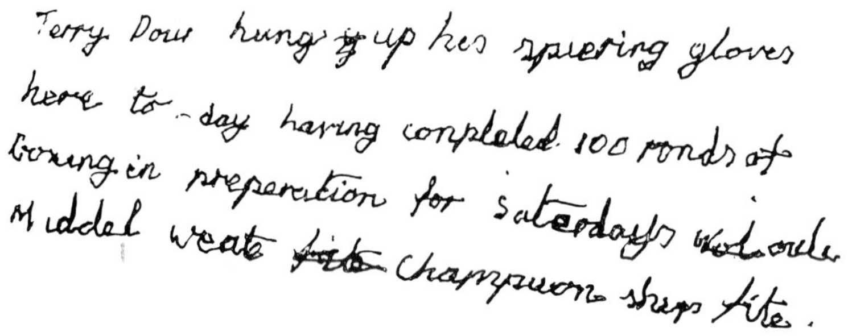

[Handwriting sample]

Terry Downs hung up his sparring gloves here today having completed 100 rounds of boxing in preparation for Saturday's world middleweight championship fight.

Fig. 19 Writing to dictation. M.K., male aged 16 years. C78625.

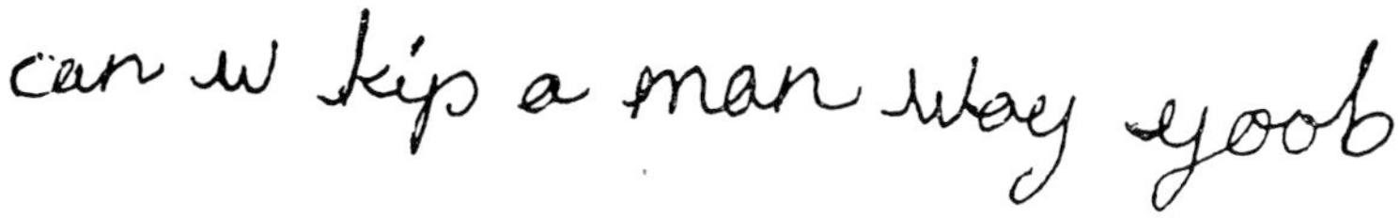

[Handwriting sample]

CAN YOU KEEP A MAN WHO WANTS TO GO?

Fig. 20 Writing to dictation. L.G., female aged 21 years. C124680.

[Handwriting sample]

Once upon a time there was a man who had a dog but no cat.

Fig. 21 Writing to dictation. L.D., female aged 12 years. A6660.

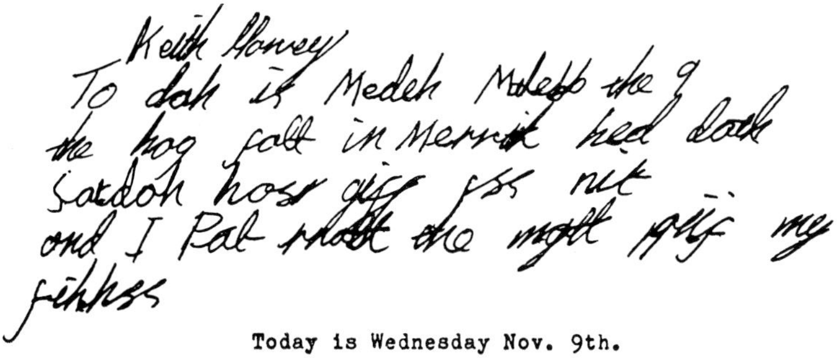

[Handwriting sample]

Today is Wednesday Nov. 9th.

They voted in America yesterday.

Saturday was Guy Fawkes' night and I set off my fireworks around the mount.

Fig. 22 Writing to dictation. K.H., male aged 12 years. I.Q. (W.I.S.C.): verbal scale 90; performance 106; full scale 97.

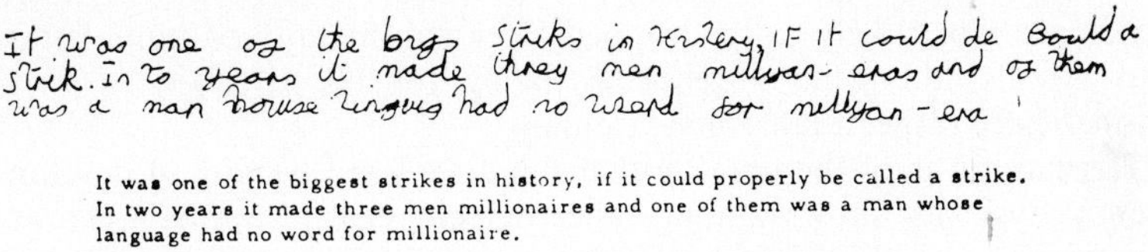

It was one of the biggest strikes in history, if it could properly be called a strike. In two years it made three men millionaires and one of them was a man whose language had no word for millionaire.

Fig. 23 Writing to dictation. C.E., male aged 11 years 10 months.

dullards. Lecours (1966) enumerated the processes of addition, deletion, substitution, and inversion, among the errors in the handwriting of dyslexics. One characteristic stressed by Hermann is the tendency by the word-blind to employ too few letters, either by telescoping words together or by dint of omission. Various examples were given. The Danish words *ner var* (now was) were represented by *nva*; *to stags* (two sorts) became *tostg*; *i naerheden* (in the vicinity) was spelt *inehed*. Illing's patient contracted the German sentence *im Hofe steht ein Schneemann* into *imhfeoscheischm*. In a Norwegian dyslexic's writing *pa primusen* (on the primus) was rendered *apmisen*. As to the letters

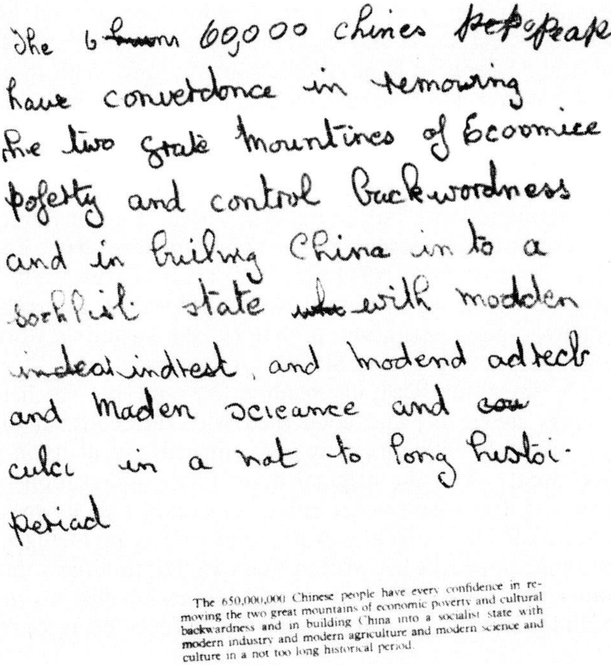

The 650,000,000 Chinese people have every confidence in removing the two great mountains of economic poverty and cultural backwardness and in building China into a socialist state with modern industry and modern agriculture and modern science and culture in a not too long historical period.

Fig. 24 Writing to dictation. A.S.K., male aged 41 years. A5440.

which are most likely to be dropped Hermann mentioned mute letters and vowels, the general tendency being for the dyslexic to write phonetically rather than conventionally.

Hermann was of the opinion that the disordered writing of developmental dyslexics shows among other defects, certain apractic characteristics. Thus a child might be able to spell aloud a word, e.g. C–A–T and then say "cat", but writes it down as "cad". The confusion of T and D was looked upon by Hermann as evidence of ideomotor apraxia. This idea must however be regarded with considerable reserve, as for example his ascription of malformed letters to an ideational apraxia.

Many of the spelling mistakes executed by a dyslexic can be explained by a resort to a homonyn, or phonetic equivalent, as when he writes KOF or COF for "cough". But not all the errors can be so interpreted. Many are quite unexpected, and some authorities, such as Miles have made a special point about the bizarre character of a dyslexic's spelling. Examples may be given: CALABRENT (celebrate), ACATION (occasion), WHELFER (welfare), CHENIL (colonel), TOENBOGEN (toboggan), FENNICHERL (financial), GINAGTIC (gigantic), CERTESE (courteous).

These graphic idiosyncrasies may depend in part upon the nature of the words dictated. When presented with a word just beyond his spelling competency, the dyslexic may make simple and understandable errors, such as straight-forward homophonic substitutions. With more unfamiliar terms, however, the dyslexic's spelling may become more and more bizarre.

Sometimes it is possible to explain some of the errors upon the basis of a defect in serial order. The dyslexic may know which letters make up a word he is about to write but he puts the letters in an incorrect sequence. Serial confusion is present, rather than simple reversal. For example the dyslexic may write NTO for "not"; VRYE for "very". When this type of defect is combined with intraverbal reversals, omission of letters, and substitution of letters, the resulting word appears most odd, as for example SAESHOW for "seashore".

As the dyslexic improves with his reading, he and his teachers become increasingly aware of, and concerned with, his conspicuous inability to spell correctly. The time may come indeed, especially in a teenager or adolescent, when the original delay in the acquisition of reading has been forgotten, and the persisting inaccuracy and slowness in reading, not realized. The problem now presents itself as an intelligent scholar who is handicapped in his written work by its untidiness and atrocious spelling. Not infrequently the case becomes labelled as one of "specific spelling defect", the background of dyslexia being overlooked.

It would be foolish to regard all educated adults who are habitual bad spellers, as having had an early background of reading-retardation.

Extreme cases, however, may well be viewed with greater suspicion. An entity labelled as "specific spelling defect" probably does not exist in isolation, but only as a sequel of a previous state of dyslexia.

The more conscientious of these ex-dyslexic scholars afflicted with spelling problems frequently resort to dictionaries in order to rectify their errors or to check their uncertainties. Unfortunately they all too often find that this is a slow and laborious task, by reason of the fact that the alphabetical serial order is not at their finger-tips. Off-hand, for example, they may not be able to say whether J comes before L, or after.

Thus a very useful clinical "test" emerges, based upon the ex-dyslexic's difficulties in rapid turning up of a name in a telephone directory. The subject is handed a bulky phone book and told to look up the number belonging to, say, "J. M. McDonald". When his performance is timed it may well emerge that 3 or 4 minutes go by before success is achieved, during which period the subject can be observed to turn over the pages this way and that in a bewildered fashion; and then, having found the appropriate first letter for the surname, he searches laboriously for the initial, starting with the letter A.

The foregoing errors in spelling are not identical with the mistakes commonly witnessed in patients who have developed an aphasia late in life. It is not correct, therefore, to speak of a "developmental dys-graphia" in this connection, as some have done. The true "dysgraphic" is an adult of at least normal education, who has developed a difficulty in expressing himself on paper as the result of disease. A study of the handwriting will show a breakdown of what had previously been a rapidly executed and highly individual motor-skill with many charac-teristics, which to a graphologist are personal and specific. Many of these revealing features will still be identifiable, despite the dysgraphia: they may even be exaggerated. The situation is quite different in the case of a developmental dyslexic who is attempting to write. No motor skill has been achieved and no individual peculiarities have developed. The situation is not so much a break-down of a consummate faculty as a failure of accomplishment.

A less well-known defect, but a highly characteristic one, is an inability on the part of the dyslexic to "spell in numbers". This is shown by a difficulty in setting down on paper to dictation long numbers entailing many digits. There may be too many noughts, or too few. Especial confusion arises over the correct placing of the commas. Thus, told to write down one hundred and forty-six, the dyslexic may put down "100,46"; for a "million and one" he may write 1,00,01 (see illustrations, for examples of other errors).

Arithmetical retardation may be associated with developmental dyslexia, but not necessarily so. Indeed, many authors and particularly

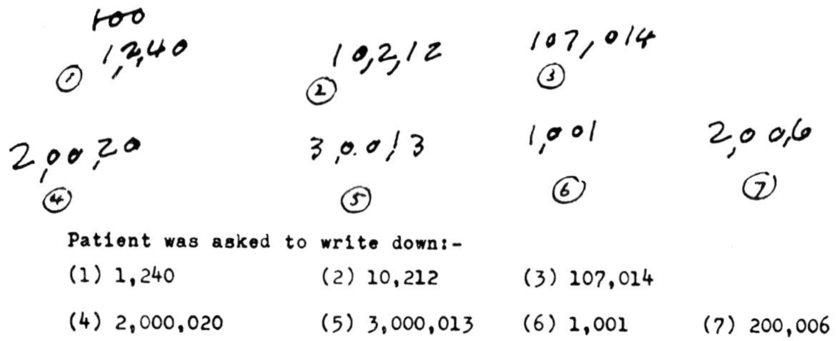
Patient was asked to write down:-
(1) 1,240
(2) 10,212
(3) 107,014
(4) 2,000,020
(5) 3,000,013
(6) 1,001
(7) 200,006

Fig. 25 Dictation of numerals. M.M., female aged 21 years.

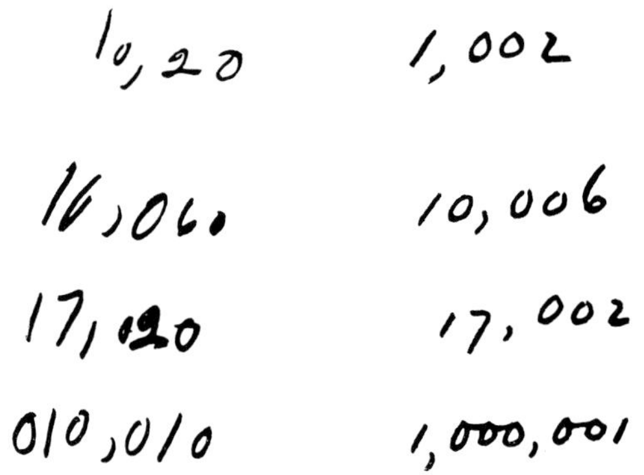

Fig. 26 Dictation of numerals (on left). T.S., male aged 11 years.

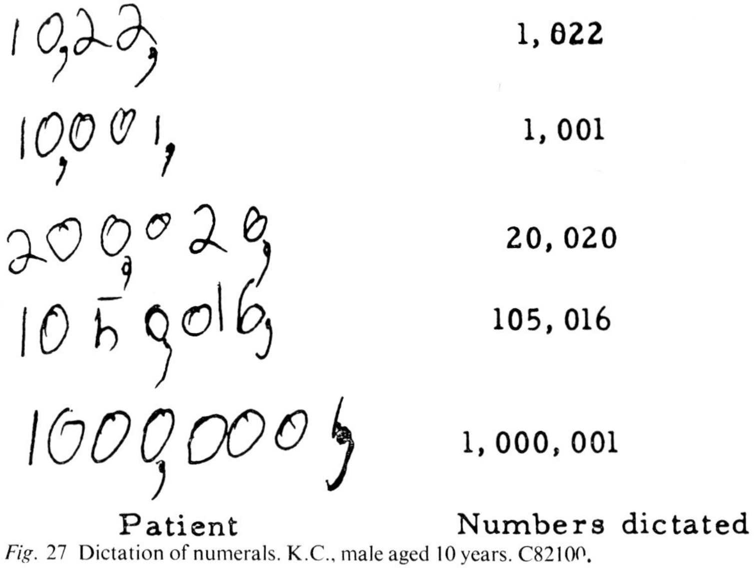
1, 022
1, 001
20, 020
105, 016
1, 000, 001
Patient
Numbers dictated

Fig. 27 Dictation of numerals. K.C., male aged 10 years. C82100.

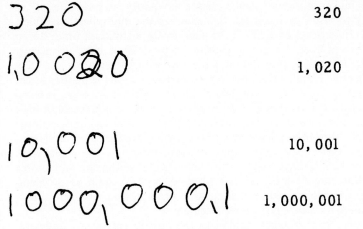

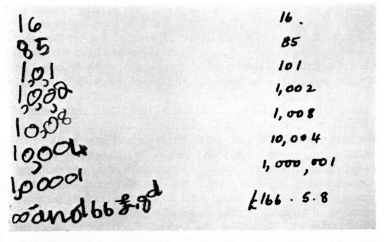

Fig. 28 Dictation of numerals. J.L., male aged 9 years. C85073.

Fig. 29 Dictation of numerals. C.C., male aged 11 years. C89235.

the earlier ones, have commented upon that paradoxical state of affairs which some of their patients have shown, in being advanced in their arithmetical prowess while grossly defective as to their ability to read. On the other hand, some writers have found that their dyslexic patients are often confused over the recognition of numerical symbols to the detriment of their powers of calculation. Difficulties in calculation may be experienced by some word-blind children for a diversity of reasons. Apart from what may be termed "number-blindness" there may exist a higher-level dyscalculia, made up partly at any rate of an inability to visualize numbers, to memorize the multiplication tables, or to retain a series of digits in the memory for a sufficient time. But in some cases at least, "mental arithmetic" is carried out with fair success, even though calculations upon paper are poorly performed. A few observers like Kopp, have, however, commented upon the mathematical skill displayed by some dyslexic patients, who may even become accountants. It is as though they were more at ease upon levels of high abstraction than with verbal symbols. "They transfer to numbers some of the pleasure others have in words". In my experience of dyslexics, however, above-average attainment in mathematics has been rare. However well he may have started with mental arithmetic and simple calculation, the dyslexic meets with a set-back as soon as problem-solving is encountered, entailing the prompt and accurate interpretation of a series of complicated sentences.

A similar inconsistency applies to the artistic abilities of dyslexics. Ordinarily their achievement is to be rated as average, while some of these children seem to be peculiarly inept as regards their drawing. In some cases at least, though certainly not all, there appears to exist no conception of perspective in their work, and it is tempting to invoke in such cases an inherent defect in spatial thought. But on the other hand some dyslexic children draw well: others indeed have excelled in their use of colour. This state of affairs has been expressly described by Bender who reproduced the pictorial art of two of her dyslexic patients. At an earlier date Kopp, who has already been quoted in association with the arithmetical abilities of dyslexics, had stated that some of these children "take a particular pleasure in a colourful world of fantasy, invent fantastic stories, and do elaborate handicraft work".

It is interesting to read a layman's view of the relationship between backwardness in reading and special aptitude in drawing and painting. M. Augustin Filon, who was tutor to the Prince Imperial, only son of the Emperor Napoleon III, found great difficulty in teaching his pupil the elements of reading, writing and spelling. But he was unusually adroit at art-work. Regarding this talent, Filon wrote: "... the astonishing gift which characterized the Prince, the memory of contours and colours, was perhaps one of the reasons that made it hard for him to attain a knowledge of spelling. When a word was pronounced to him, he saw in his mind's eye the man or the thing, and not a printed word". (*Memoirs of the Prince Imperial* (1856–1879) by Augustin Filon. Heinemann, London, 1913, p. 46.)

In 1954 a German newspaper carried the story of Jack Taylor, an uneducated, dyslexic Englishman of 24 years who was found to be a talented painter of promise. A successful exhibition of his work was held at the Redfern Gallery. At school he had been quite unable to learn to read.

In my series of 125 alleged dyslexics, I have encountered 17 cases where artistic merit I rated as slightly above average. More often the spontaneous drawings are best described as immature: sometimes a trifle bizarre. Not infrequently they are unusually small, and often the sketch is not placed boldly in the centre of the sheet of paper, but is relegated either to one corner, or to the very bottom of the page.

One of the routine tasks set to a putative dyslexic is to draw a bicycle. This test is a useful one for it often brings to the surface an underlying spatio-constructional disorder. In four of my cases, the sketch was executed in an unusual fashion, being in the nature of a bird's-eye view. (See Fig. 30.)

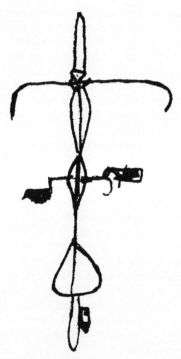

Fig. 30 Spontaneous plan drawing of a bicycle executed by a hyperkinetic putative dyslexic boy of 9 years and 7 months, with a family history of dyslexia. Reading age 12·09; spelling age 9. I.Q. 149 (Stanford-Binet).

Chapter VII
Perceptual problems

Ophthalmological aspects

Refractive errors play no part in the aetiology of developmental dyslexia. Campion (1965) stressed that poor visual acuity is rarely a deterrent in learning to read, even though "slow but accurate readers" may be given a boost by acquiring glasses which improve their visual acuity for near objects. But such a group probably did not include dyslexics. Campion went on shrewdly to state that the improved performance among his slow readers was probably due to psychological reasons.

Furthermore it may be asserted that developmental dyslexia is not the product of muscle-imbalance or imperfect binocular fusion, despite the association noted, or the causal importance claimed by Betts (1936), Eames (1932–48) and others, between reading-disability and such visual defects as heterophoria, fusion anomalies, field restriction and hypermetropia. No correlation exists between the degree of binocular co-ordination and reading ability (Gruber, 1962). The problem as to whether the perception of visual sense-data is disturbed will be discussed more fully later.

It has been contended that dyslexia is rare in one-eyed children (including those blinded in one eye, or with an amblyopia (*ex anopsia*). How this idea arose, and where the statistical data are to be found, is not easy to determine. Indeed dyslexic children have at times been "treated" by obscuring the non-dominant eye with a patch. (Benton Jnr., 1968). Bellman *et al.* (1967) found 3 uniocular amblyopic children within their series of 47 dyslexics, and 2 out of a group of 58 good readers. To date therefore both the assertion and the rationale stand upon an insecure and uncontrolled premiss.

Minor upsets in the discrimination of colours, or perhaps merely in their correct naming, have been mentioned by a number of writers, particularly in Germany (e.g. Warburg, 1911; Laubenthal, 1936; Pflugfelder, 1948). In my own series of 11 cases of retarded readers I have found 100 cases of partial colour-blindness, the percentage probably being non-significant.

Very occasionally a young dyslexic may give evidence of what would appear to be a selective kind of inverted vision. This may be suggested by the manner in which they gaze at illustrations in a picture-book, or by their habit of drawing in an upside down fashion.

> Thus J.S., an intelligent little boy of 5 years and 1 month had been observed often, though not always, to hold a book upside down. He would usually put the shoes on the wrong feet, and his

TOP

DOOR

HOUSE

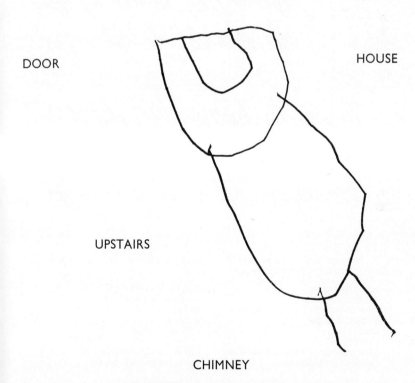

UPSTAIRS

CHIMNEY

Fig. 31 Drawing of a house executed by a very intelligent boy of 5 years and 1 month, referred to me because of "inverted vision". He would hold a book upside down to look at the illustrations, and would draw in the same manner. There was a strong family history of dyslexia. A follow-up report four years later indicated that this boy too was now obviously dyslexic, but he had lost his "inverted vision".

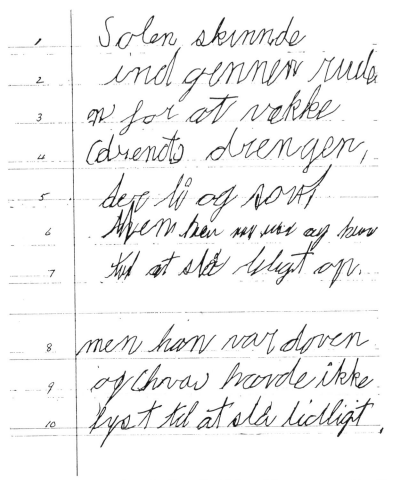

Fig. 32 Inverted writing by an intelligent Danish boy of 10 years, presumably with dyslexia, executed with the right hand.

Solen skinnede	The sun was shining
ind gennem rude	through the pane
n for at vaekke	to wake
(drend) drengen,	the boy
der lå og sov	who was asleep
Men han var doven og havde ikke	But he was lazy and had no
lyst til at stå tidligt op.	desire for getting up early.
men han var doven	but he was lazy
og (hva) havde ikke	and had no
lyst til at stå tidligt (op).	desire for getting up early.

Lines 1 to 5, and lines 8 to 10, were written with the sheet of paper turned upside down. The word (drend) in line 4, and the word (hva) in line 9 represent mis-spellings corrected by the boy.

vest back to front. When examined in my consulting room he was observed often to gaze at a picture in an inverted fashion, and frequently sideways. His drawings of a man, house and bicycle were drawn in an inverted fashion. (See Fig. 31.) The four component parts of a jigsaw puzzle were assembled sideways on. Kohs' blocks were put together correctly except that the pattern was rotated through 90 degrees. When given a watch he handled it upside down, but he could not tell the time. In this case there was a strong family history of developmental dyslexia.

The question may be posed whether more searching ocular examinations might perhaps uncover certain subtle defects, but whether these should be looked upon as the product or the cause of the dyslexia, would also require an answer. Thus Lesèvre *et al.* have been measuring the reaction-time preceding willed movements of the eyes to command, in normals and in dyslexics. Certain standards were established, including the observation that the latency of movements to the right differed slightly from that of movements to the left. In dyslexic children not only were all eye-movements slower in initiation, but the usual difference between right and left ocular deviation was not present.

Of more immediate importance is the question as to the nature of reading-movements of the eyes in dyslexics as compared with normals.

The interesting topic of the character of the ocular movements performed by normal persons and others during the act of reading, has been studied by various techniques including photographic, electro-encephalographic and scopographic. Considerable variation occurs from one individual to another; depending upon a diversity of factors such as for example the length of the lines; the size of the type; and in particular the content of the text and the words entailed. Among the personal determinants which seem to be important are the age, and more especially the cultural and intellectual status of the subject. Ophthalmographic studies may therefore adduce important objective information as to a person's efficiency in reading. Such studies take note of the number and duration of pauses (fixations, or *stations du regard*); the number and amplitude of regressions (or backward movements of the eyes); the span of words encompassed by each sweep; and the rate of comprehension. Depending upon the character of the eye-movements is the overall rate of reading. Ordinarily a reader absorbs a printed page by identifying either single words or phrases; or groups of letters; or perhaps only individual letters at a time, according to the degree of familiarity of the reader with his material; his skill or practice; and the inherent clarity or obscurity of the text. According to Matjecek* normal Czech children of the age of 10 can

*Personal communication.

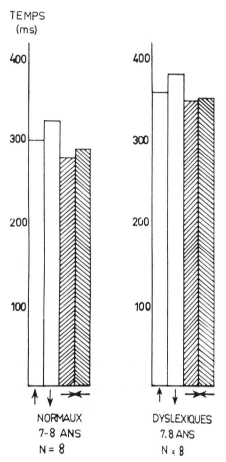

Fig. 33 Measurement of the reaction-time preceding willed movements of the eyes up, down, to the right and to the left, in normal children and in dyslexics. (After Lesèvre *et al.*)

read about 110 words a minute. Most adults manage about 300 words per minute. A few gifted readers can cope with 1,000 words per minute, or even more. One young prodigy in Taylor's series mastered as many as 2,200 words per minute. Most college professors, he found, did not read more than 350 or at the most 500 words in a minute. The aptitude improves in rate and quality with age and education (see Table II, p. 57), and, as is well known, the reading rate can be considerably enhanced by dint of special techniques of training.

Ocular movements are naturally altered in certain pathological conditions like hemianopia, the pattern differing according to whether

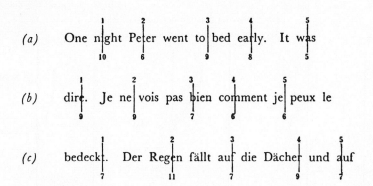

Examples of eye-movement records in three languages: (a) a college student in the United States[3]; (b) an efficient reader of French;[4] (c) a native German reader.[5] In this and the following figure, the vertical lines represent centres of fixations. The number above the lines indicate the serial order of fixations; those below indicate duration in thirtieths of a second.

Fig. 34 Records of eye movements during the act of reading. (After Gray.)

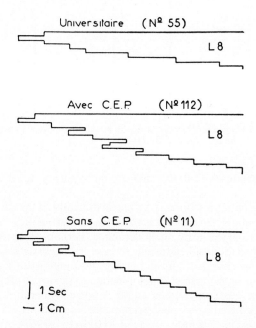

Fig. 35 Scopographic records made from three subjects with different educational backgrounds presented with the same text (line 8. *soir de Vendange*). (1) Reader on the staff of a University; (2) Reader who was a certified student; (3) Reader who had not yet attained the certified student status. (After Rémond *et al.*)

56	*The dyslexic child*

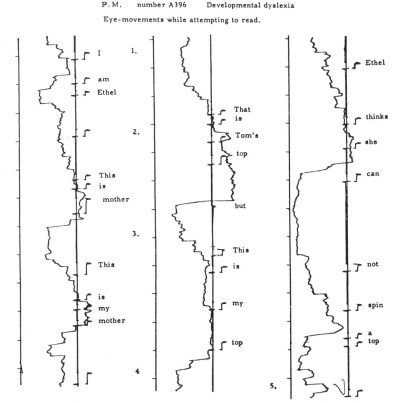

P.M.   number A396   Developmental dyslexia

Eye-movements while attempting to read.

Fig. 36 Record of eye movements during the act of attempting to read, in a dyslexic. P.M., aged 31. A396. (Courtesy of Dr. Hallpike.)

the homonymous visual loss lies to the right or to the left of the midline.

In aphasic patients who have an alexic difficulty in the comprehension of verbal symbols, the movements of the eyes during the act of attempting to read are necessarily much deranged. Perhaps this subject has not yet been sufficiently studied for one to interpret these defects completely.

As might be expected, unusual ocular movements during attempts at reading occur in the case of developmental dyslexics. Unfortunately the material that has been studied so far is not considerable. At one time it was asserted that abnormal eye movements were the actual cause of backwardness in learning to read. Hildreth (1963), for example, alleged that "reversals of letter-sequence in perceiving certain words are due to faulty eye movements". Witty and Kopel (1936) stated that left eye dominance in some cases results in the eyes moving from right

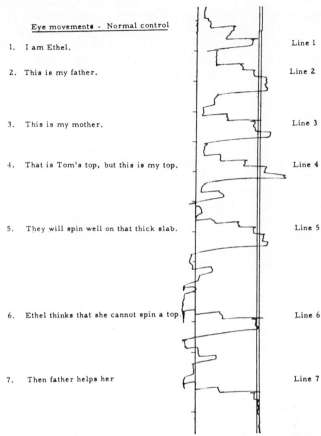

1.   I am Ethel.   Line 1

2.   This is my father.   Line 2

3.   This is my mother.   Line 3

4.   That is Tom's top, but this is my top.   Line 4

5.   They will spin well on that thick slab.   Line 5

6.   Ethel thinks that she cannot spin a top.   Line 6

7.   Then father helps her   Line 7

Fig. 37 Eye movements during the act of reading the same text as by the patient P.M. Normal control. (Courtesy of Dr. Hallpike.)

TABLE II. *Measurable Components of the Fundamental Reading Skill.*

GRADE LEVEL	1st	2nd	3rd	4th	5th	6th	Jr. HS	HS	College
Fixations per 100 words	240	200	170	136	118	105	95	83	75
Regressions per 100 words	55	45	37	30	26	23	18	15	11
Average span of recognition (in words)	0·42	0·50	0·59	0·73	0·85	0·95	1·05	1·21	1·33
Average duration of fixation (in seconds)	0·33	0·30	0·26	0·24	0·24	0·24	0·24	0·24	0·23
Average rate of comprehension (in words per minute)	75	100	138	180	216	235	255	296	340

Compiled by Taylor (1957) from over 5000 eye-movement records.

to left during the act of reading, presumably causing difficulty or delay in comprehension. Mosse and Daniels (1959), who described a particular defect in the return sweep from the end of one line to the start of the next ("linear dyslexia"), went on to assert that anomalies in this manoeuvre are responsible for difficulty in comprehension, arising in turn from faulty habits of reading which are psychologically determined.

But arguments of this kind are surely topsy-turvy. Faulty eye-movements must be regarded as the outcome of a difficulty in reading, and not its cause. An analogy with the disordered reading movements of the eyes shown by aphasic subjects can be fairly made. A possible exception to this statement may be found in the curious group of cases described by Prechtl and Stemmer (1959, 1962). Out of a series of children with learning difficulties, a distinct neurological syndrome was identified in 50 cases. These children showed clumsiness combined with choreiform movements. In 96 % of them the eye muscles were involved, leading to disturbances of conjugate movement and difficulty in fixation and reading. The authors alleged that the chorea caused both difficulty in mental concentration and also in fixation during the act of reading. Obviously this report bears little or no relationship to the problem of specific developmental dyslexia.

The thesis of Mlle. Lesèvre (1964) on eye-movements is of particular importance in this connection, although the total number of dyslexics in her series was only 22. The author found that these poor readers showed more ocular instability than in her controls, as well as a slower oculomotor reaction-time, and a greater number of short pauses, and *mouvements oculaires inutiles*. Consistent unilateral scanning, whether from left to right or from right to left, did not occur, a subject which will be discussed in a later chapter. Mlle. Lesèvre did not ascribe the poor oculomotor performance to inexperience, nor to incorrect teaching, nor to reading-habits.

Although disordered ocular movements must be looked upon as the result of reading-difficulties, and not their cause, the inco-ordination can be controlled by certain manoeuvres. These may help the poor reader—obviously not by assisting comprehension of the subject-matter—but by facilitating the task at a peripheral level. Perhaps some measure of fatigue is thereby avoided. Thus a marker placed just beneath the line under scrutiny will prevent the gaze wandering down to other lines where perhaps a familiar word will distract attention. This same trick will also help to guide the poor reader from the end of one line to the start of the next.

When a dyslexic is presented with two identical texts which are just within his power of comprehension, one being printed in large type and the other in a lower case, he may make a surprising choice. Thus he may assert that he finds it easier to read the smaller print. This is perhaps so because more letters to a line entail fewer eye-movements, as well as less frequent switches from one line to the next. Dyslexics do not always make such a choice: some seem happier with the larger typology; others—perhaps the majority—express themselves as indifferent.

The notion that faulty eye-movements play an important inhibitory role in learning to read has led to a vogue for remedial eye-exercises in the management of a dyslexic. This practice, commoner in America than in Great Britain, and now less often carried out than was the case a few years ago, is empirically dubious and scientifically suspect. Goldberg's discussion (1968) is an important corrective to a great deal of loose orthoptic thinking. "Defective vision and muscle imbalance" he wrote "do not have a significant role in the etiology of a condition that is influenced by cognitive learning ... Muscle imbalance and strabismus do not affect the interpretation of symbols by the brain". The work of Smith (1966) was quoted by Goldberg to the effect that patterns of eye-movement may be facilitated by appropriate exercises but no improvement in comprehension results.

Closely bound up with the subject of eye-movements in the act of reading is the question of the rate of identification of verbal symbols when studied tachistoscopically.

Normal subjects, according to Gray, are able to identify at a single short exposure four or five unrelated letters, but four or five times that number of letters when they constitute meaningful words. But the number of symbols perceived at each exposure depends not entirely upon the extent to which the material "makes sense". In the case of words, certain letters are perceived more quickly than others, e.g. letters with a distinctive shape, or those which extend above or below the horizontal line. Such letters attract particular attention, and supply clues for the recognition of the word as a whole.

Tachistoscopic testing was applied to patients with developmental dyslexia by Bachmann (1927). Normal and dyslexic children were shown words both meaningful and meaningless, and words with or without sound-pictures. Exposures were of 0·2 sec., 0·5 sec. and 1 sec., beginning with short words (i.e. of three or four letters) and increasing to words composed of so many letters that reading became impossible. His findings caused him surprise. It was found that the limit of readability was reached with the same number of letters in the case of dyslexics and normal children alike. However, the number of letters in the words entailed was small. The rate of reading was found to be diminished in the dyslexics under tachistoscopic testing, and this applied both to real words and to nonsense combinations of letters.

Tachistoscopic studies carried out by Schilder (1944) upon seven subjects showed that difficulty in perception was usually confined to letters and words, and did not entail numerical symbols. Four-digit numbers were identified, whereas four-letter words were not. Pictures were readily recognized and there was no trace of mirror-mistakes. The accuracy of picture-recognition contrasted markedly with the difficulties and delays in word-recognition. When verbal symbols were presented tachistoscopically, no increase in the difficulty of recognition resulted. Schilder drew some important conclusions from these data. The situation seemed to be quite unlike what was found in the acquired alexics of adulthood, where the difficulty in perception was a pure optical product. But in the case of the developmental dyslexic (or congenital word-blind, as he said) . . . "the difficulty concerns the inner structure of the word and its sounds. It is an agnostic trouble, not so much concerning the merely optic sphere, but a sphere which is nearer to the intellectual life than the optic perception. It is true that every gnostic function is also an intellectual one, but the intellectual function which is disturbed in the congenital reading-disability cases is of a higher level than the function which is disturbed in the cases of pure word-blindness".

From this point Schilder went on to examine the probable nature of the essential defect in cases of developmental dyslexia, a matter which will be discussed later.

Obviously questions of whether the optic perception of verbal symbols is deranged in dyslexics, and if so in what manner, go right to the heart of the problem.

The early researches of Fildes (1921) into the fundamental nature of dyslexia constitute an early and important contribution. "Word-blindness" was, for her, but one aspect of a more general—yet still specific—defect in either the visual or the auditory regions of the brain, or in both. The dyslexic's failure to associate and retain sounds and forms, lies to some extent in this primary defect. Forms or sounds consequently fail to become meaningful. Whether there is also a failure in primary retention and in the formation of memory-images she could not determine.

Fildes' conclusions are interesting, but they are unfortunately marred by the fact that 25 out of her 26 cases were children of low intelligence (I.Q. 50 to 82). Nevertheless in her series she found no close relationship between the intellectual level and the power of reading. Analysis of her patients' performances showed that the inability to read depended upon a specific rather than a general defect. Tests for visual discrimination and for retention of nonsense-forms revealed an impairment among dyslexics far beyond the normal, though there was no lack of speed in perception, nor any failure to recognize the various forms. Fildes concluded that slowness in visual perception is not an important factor in reading difficulties. Non-readers as a class do not find it easy to distinguish between visual impressions which closely resemble each other, although they can readily appreciate and retain differences which are greater in degree. The failure is due partly to an inability to retain the visual impressions and partly to slowness of association-processes which hinder the finding of the appropriate name.

Fildes also found that her non-readers as a group displayed a reduction of auditory power, less severe, however, than in the realm of visual function. Incidentally, this is the first point in the history of the dyslexia-problem where auditory factors have been raised for discussion.

When tested with random artificial associations between names and Greek letters, dyslexics found this task even harder, allegedly because the symbols were so very like each other. This finding supported the conclusion that had already been drawn, namely that it is difficult to forge linkages between names and forms *unless these latter are distinctive in appearance*. This factor should be borne in mind when the question is discussed whether teachers should adopt artificial systems such as the initial training alphabet (i.t.a.).

Non-readers in Fildes' series made associations between meaningless words and meaningful forms as readily as normal readers, but their difficulties increased as both forms and sounds grew less distinctive. "Forms and sounds must be readily distinguishable, and both must be meaningful. The essential defect in dyslexia seems to be a failure of forms or sounds to achieve meaning".

Fildes' work suggests that a pictorial "test" such as the one devised by Maruyama, might conceivably be of diagnostic assistance in dyslexics. A series of non-verbal symbols, differing in their spatial orientation, and graduating in complexity, are exposed and then matched from a duplicate set. The child is instructed to match the individual cards after the lapse of a short period of time, the model being removed from sight. In my experience with this test, dyslexics score well, and I no longer employ this manoeuvre as a routine.

Developmental dyslexics usually show no difficulty whatsoever in such non-verbal tasks as discriminating between pictures of different types of automobiles, aircraft, flowers, or dogs. Nor do they fail to identify photographs of such celebrities as might be expected to be within their experience. Ordinarily there is no trouble in recognizing traffic signs. The question of musical notation is more complex, and is discussed later. It seems likely therefore that defective pattern-learning cannot be the sole factor or even the most significant one in the explanation of dyslexia.

Vernon (1957) in studying backwardness in reading, could not find in her cases evidence of any general disorder of the visual perception of shapes. Some deficiency in the accurate discrimination of detail and also of spatial orientation was possible, related perhaps to a general lack of maturation in analysis and in visual memory. She believed, however, that these defects were likely to be the result of the reading disability, and not the cause. Vernon was studying a widely ranged series of cases where reading skill was slow or retarded, and at that time she explicitly objected to the conception of a specific dyslexia. Her conclusions as to the role of visual perception are important none the less, for her series almost certainly included subjects whom a neurologist would regard as developmental dyslexics. It would be interesting in this connection to employ Benton's visual retention test in a large series of dyslexics.

In some ways, the results of the various special tests of high visuo-psychic functions in dylexics have been contradictory. The accomplishment of the Bender Visual Motor Gestalt test has been noted as inferior when performed by dyslexics (Galifret-Gonjon, 1952). Goins (1958) claimed that there was a correlation between poor reading and defective visual form-perception and insecure directional orientation. Lachmann (1960) also found that some dyslexics performed the Bender Visual Motor Gestalt test poorly. Negative findings emerged, however, from the work of Bachmann (1927), Ombredane (1937) and Malmquist (1958). Benton was probably correct when he shrewdly pointed out that when visuo-psychic defects were demonstrable in dyslexics, it is only so in the case of the younger subjects. He concluded therefrom, that deficiency in visual form-perception is *not* an important correlate of developmental dyslexia. This is supported by my experience that dyslexics cope well with the Maruyama test.

Yet another method of exploring higher visual discrimination which has been applied to retarded readers, is by way of an "embedded figures test" such as the one devised by Gottschaldt. One or two simple geometric figures are presented, together with a number of very complex designs. (See Fig. 38.) The testee is required to detect which of the simple figures lies concealed or incorporated within the complex design. The problem is therefore one of holding or isolating simple patterns in elaborate configurations, a task which is notoriously difficult for patients with parieto-occipital lesions. Tjossem *et al.* applied this manoeuvre to a series of 16 slow readers and 16 able readers, and the scores were 10·7 and 13·1 respectively. They concluded that this embedded figure test discriminates between able and slow readers at the age-range 7 to 9 years.

Audiological aspects

Although simple deafness plays no part in the aetiology of specific developmental dyslexia, it is understandable that any child with a mild hearing defect may experience some difficulty in learning to read. The problem of associating verbal sounds with their graphic or printed counterparts, is likely to be hindered if the child does not always accurately perceive the acoustic properties of speech. Lloyd Thompson pointed out that most children learn to spell "by ear" because they lack a clear-cut visual memory-pattern of words. If in addition they have no absolutely precise hearing of words, their handicap increases. In this

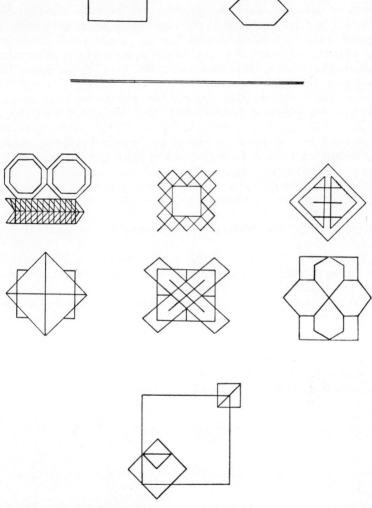

Fig. 38 The Gottschaldt figure test.

way it may happen that mild and often undetected degrees of deafness are more productive of learning difficulties than are severe losses of hearing. Consequently in embarking upon the somewhat intricate task of identifying cases of developmental dyslexia, it is often necessary to test the child audiometrically.

Even in those cases which are presumed to be examples of developmental dyslexia, it is necessary to probe the factor of auditory perception somewhat deeper. From questions of hypoacusis one can turn to forms of dysacusis. Even though there may exist no demonstrable deafness, and no restriction in the audiometric scale—peripheral or central—some qualitative disorder may be present which handicaps the accurate perception of speech. Just as in certain cases of acquired aphasia in the adult, there may conceivably be a "dysphonemia" or confusion between consonantal and vocalic sounds of somewhat similar nature e.g. *lid* and *lit*, *bed* and *bad*. The routine assessment of children with presumed dyslexia should therefore include some modification of Wepman's test. That is to say, the child should be instructed to repeat a series of pairs of words, or even nonsense syllables, quietly but clearly enunciated. Examples include pairs like *mummy, nunny; street, sleet; dock, dog; bap, pap; slim, slam; tin, ten;* and so on. The patient's head should be turned away so that he does not receive clues by dint of lip-reading. Sometimes the words proferred should be identical, like *cat, cat*. It is wise not to include in the list too many rhyming words, for children are particularly apt to seize on and identify such pairs.

The question of auditory attention may also require investigation, for the act of concentration upon a sequence of nearly identical sounds may prove difficult to some dyslexics.

Yet another complicated language test, which includes the factor of auditory memory, is to have the patient recite back to the examiner the theme of a simple story. A word-for-word recapitulation is not required so long as the gist of the tale is given. This test has the added advantage of indicating the testee's command of abstraction and linguistic expression, aspects of language which are occasionally defective in the larger community of poor readers.

Chapter VIII
Cerebral dominance

That many dyslexic children were not strongly right-handed subjects was realized early in the history of "congenital word blindness". With the passage of time increasing importance became attached to this aspect of the problem, and it seemed more and more evident that dyslexic children often lacked a firm and determinate left cerebral dominance. The occurrence of reversals in writing and reading still further directed attention to this problem and a powerful impetus was afforded by the observations of Orton starting from 1925.

Some authors have noted a high incidence of frank left-handedness. Thus, sinistrality was observed in 75% of the cases recorded by Roudinesco, Trelat and Trelat; and in 29% of Dearborn's series. Wall (1945, 1946) found that 29% of his dyslexics were left-handers as opposed to 14% in a control series. Of Kågen's cases, 15% were left-handed, as compared with 4% among controls. Findings such as these at once throw doubt upon the propriety of the suggestion put forward in 1906 by Claiborne, that dyslexic children should actually be taught to become left-handed. Many other writers, however, could not satisfy themselves that there was a greater incidence of left-handedness among the community of poor readers (Monroe, Eames, Gates, Gates and Bond, Witty and Kopel, Bennet, Jackson, Hallgren). Others attached less importance to the role of left-handedness than to left-eyedness, a feature which was found in 27% of Skydsgaard's (as opposed to 21% in his controls); 40% in Kågen's series (32% in controls); and 100% in Macmeeken's 383 patients. Of the last-named group only 4 were left-handed. Monroe, Dearborn and Crosland also found a higher incidence of left-eyed subjects among poor readers.

Mixed laterality was then imagined to be a factor of special importance in dyslexics who might, for example, prove to be left-eyed, right-handed and left-footed. Any such combination might occur. Thus Orton found mixed eye-hand dominance in 69 out of his 102 cases. Monroe, Dearborn, Eames and Skydsgaard also found a greater proportion of poor readers displaying mixed dominance. But these observations were not confirmed by Gates and Bond, Bennet, Wolfe, Hildreth, Kågen or Hallgren, the last-named commenting upon the inadequacies of most accepted tests of eyedness.

Other writers again have regarded many dyslexics as being "ambi-dextrous". But nowadays the notion of ambidexterity is realized as being far more complex than hitherto. Eisenson prefers to speak of a person as being, not ambidextrous, but rather as "ambi-non-dextrous", while many use the term "ambilevity" rather than "ambidexterity". In any case the inference is that there exists in such individuals no clear-cut dominance of one hemisphere over another. In this respect inadequate cerebral dominance and mixed laterality may be considered together, both representing a failure to achieve a strong left cerebral suzerain. This may indeed prove to be a factor of greater significance in the aetiology of dyslexia than sinistrality itself, whether latent or overt. Thus out of Harris's series of dyslexics (1957), 40% showed mixed dominance (18% in controls) and 25% mixed handedness (8·2% in controls). Of the Chesni cases, 37% showed imperfect laterality. As Granjon-Galifret and Ajuriaguerra put it (1951), "dyslexics are not more often left-handed than normals, but they are more often badly lateralised".

Orton believed that during the normal processes of early visual education, storage of memory-images of letters and words takes place in both hemispheres, and that with the first efforts at learning to read, external visual stimuli irradiate equally into the associative cortices of both hemispheres, and are there represented in both dextrad and sinistrad fashion. The process of learning to read entails the elision from the focus of attention of the confusing memory-images of the non-dominant hemisphere which are in reversed form-order, as well as the selection of those which are in correct orientation and sequence. In cases of reading-disability the memory-patterns in the non-dominant hemisphere are incompletely suppressed.

Although this over-simple hypothesis might not find favour in contemporary thinking, the underlying notion of imperfect cerebral dominance is still acceptable today as one factor of importance.

The determination of cerebral dominance is a far more complicated matter than generally realized. It is often difficult to determine handedness especially in a youngster under the age of 10 years. The tests which are utilized differ widely in physiological validity. Some entail motor skills which again may be ordained by convention. Thus a natural sinistral may be taught to write with the other hand and to manipulate a spoon and fork in the traditional manner. With some cultures a veritable taboo exists regarding the use of the left hand at meals. However much he may feel inclined to favour the left, a Chinese is not allowed to use chopsticks except with the right hand, nor is a Hindu permitted to feed himself with the fingers of the left (unclean) hand. Some motor skills are outside the scope of such prejudices, e.g. throwing a ball, or using a nail brush. This latter manoeuvre is one of the most useful indices of handedness, except in very young children who are often maladroit and unpractised in manipulating a brush. Many sinistrals find themselves compelled to adopt unnatural right-handed techniques simply because certain tools are manufactured for dextrad use, e.g. scissors, bradawls. While it is possible to purchase left-handed golf clubs, this does not apply to hockey sticks. Some "tests" have the merit of being almost entirely "automatic", e.g. the manner of clasping hands, of folding the arms, or of holding hands behind the back. Unfortunately these particular manœuvres are of somewhat limited value and the correlation with cerebral dominance does not appear to be high. Bimanual activities also need to be investigated. While left-handed card-dealing is common enough in dextrad subjects, a sinistral might be expected to hold a spade or a baseball bat in the fashion which suits him best. Again teaching may ordain a manner of motor behaviour which is "unnatural" as when a sinistral schoolboy is not permitted by his coach to wield a cricket bat in a left-handed fashion.

Children often show a discrepancy between the two lower limbs as regards kicking and hopping. Perhaps most young subjects prefer to kick with the right foot but to hop on the left. The sinistral may perhaps choose to get on his bicycle by swinging his left leg over the machine, but his riding master probably would not permit him to mount a pony in that fashion.

Common tests for eyedness comprise the observation of the eye preferred for gazing through a telescope or microscope, or for aiming a rifle. Some, however, make a distinction between the "sighting" eye and the "controlling" eye, and furthermore isolate a group of subjects with a mixed control due to alternating intermittent macular suppression. If visual acuity differs in the two eyes, then the subject usually, but not necessarily, uses the better eye for sighting.

It follows from what has been said that there is no easy road to determining cerebral dominance. Wada's technique is of course valuable in determining which hemisphere is the more concerned with the faculty of speech, but this can scarcely be regarded as suitable for routine employment. Batteries of simple clinical tests have been devised by Harris, by Hull, by Černáček, amongst others, but the constituent items of these batteries are not of equal value. If, as the result of research upon a wide enough scale, it ever became possible to assess each individual test, then it might eventually become possible to construct a sort of "dominance quotient", and by means of a formula, to conclude that the testee is for example 80% left-brained and 20% right-brained, rather than one with a straight-forward left cerebral dominance.

A simple morphological index of handedness (or cerebral dominance), is sorely needed, one which could be applied, if necessary, to a cadaver. In the past, attempts have been made to identify the preferred upper limb by comparing the venular pattern on the backs of the hands, or the relative vascularity of the finger-nail beds. The data have not been convincing enough for general acceptance.

Carlos Mendilaharsu* has been in the habit of using a series of

*Personal communication.

tests for handedness and footedness which depend upon the factor of muscle-tonus. In his experience a relative hypotonia affects the limbs of the non-preferred side, leading to a passive hyperextensibility of, for example, the thumb, as well as a hyperflexibility of the forearm at the elbow joint, and of the whole lower limb. (See Figs. 39 (a) and (b).)

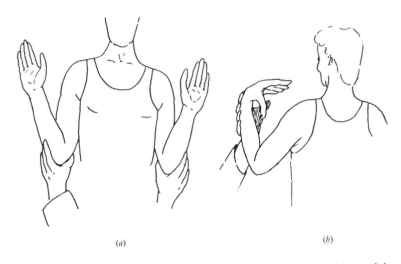

(a)   (b)

Fig. 39 Tests for handedness, as devised by André-Thomas and elaborated by Economos and Dimo, and later still by Mendilaharsu. "Extensibility", or range of passive movement, is greater on the non-dominant side. For example, in (a) the elbow-joint can be passively bent to a greater degree on the left, i.e. the non-dominant arm. (b) The same greater range of extensibility is shown on the left side where the thumb can be pressed closer to the forearm than on the right (i.e. the preferred) hand.

An unusual "test" for handedness has been suggested by Friedman (1952), depending upon the position of the hair-whorl. He estimated the percentage for a right whorl in a normal community to be 21%, and for a left whorl 70%. Applying this sign to a series of retarded readers, Tjossem, Hansen and Ripley (1962) found a right whorl in 54%, and a left whorl in 21%. These differences were regarded as significant, and the figures, it was suggested, pointed to an abnormal tendency to congenital right laterality, despite the fact that the majority of the children were right-handed.*

* A right hair whorl was found in 36 (25 left cerebral dominance; 8 right cerebral dominance; 3 ambidexters). In 27 a left hair whorl was found (23 left cerebral dominance; 2 right cerebral dominance; 2 ambidexters). The hair whorl was centrally placed in 37 children (27 left cerebral dominance; 5 right cerebral dominance; 3 ambidexters).

Even this problem is more complicated than might appear, however. A study of a sufficiently large series shows that mere inspection of the scalp cannot always determine for certain the location of the hair-whorl. Some persons have two hair-whorls, close to each other, one on either side of the sagittal plane. Others cannot be said to have a whorl so much as a short transverse slit which runs either horizontally or slightly tilted, across the vertex. Some authors believe that the significant factor to be noted in the case of a hair-whorl is not so much its sidedness, as its inherent direction, i.e. whether the hairs curve in a clockwise or anti-clockwise fashion. The former type of patterning is by far the commoner, and indeed I have yet to see an anti-clockwise formation in any child with a reading problem. Obviously we need to know much more about this anatomical subject in the general community.

Dominance of one or other occipital lobe may not necessarily correlate with total hemispheric superiority. The impression has grown up that in the recognition of common objects the right temporal visual field is more efficient than the left field. Perhaps it would be better to say that the right lateral field is the "preferred" rather than the "superior" one, during such manoeuvres as a visual sweep of distant tangentially located objects. Furthermore there has been a tendency to correlate this so-called right lateralization with right-handedness. Some have believed that preferential scanning from left to right is the result of practice in reading; others believe that the lateralization is independent of reading, and antecedant to its acquirement. Some even go further and associate a difficulty in learning to read conventional left to right European textual matter, as opposed to Hebrew, Hindu, Arabic, with an innate lateralization from right to left.

This idea may well be an over-simplification, however, and in the case of reading-matter it may be the beginning part of the word and its position in relation to the fixation point which is all-important. Nevertheless, the preferred direction of automatic lateral gaze is well worth noting during the routine examination of dyslexics, when drawing tentative conclusions as to cerebral dominance. A simple test-procedure consists in a horizontal row of circles of various colours, displayed directly facing the subject who is then directed to enumerate the different colours (see Fig. 40). The child usually proceeds to identify

Fig. 40 Pink, blue, orange, yellow, black, green, brown, red, dark blue.

the colours from left to right.* Thus in a series of 100 presumed dyslexics in whom this test was carried out the results were as follows:

	Total	Mainly RIGHT c. dom.	Mainly LEFT c. dom.	Ambi-dextrous	Eyedness	
					r.	L
Left → Right	76	8	61	7	46	30
Right → Left	16	2	11	3	7	9
Ambiguous	8	1	7	0	3	5

Control figures are needed but these findings suggest that presumed dyslexics do not differ from what probably occurs among normal readers as regards the direction of their preferred lateral gaze.

This would differ from the findings of McFie, and also Ettlinger and Jackson. These authors found on the basis of the Jasper-Raney-Phi test, which compares the illusory movement of objects within the two homonymous visual fields, that dyslexics show no clear-cut directional preponderance. This suggests a lack of one-sided occipital dominance which again may indicate a non-maturation. This state of "cerebral ambilaterality" is believed by some to be associated with an unstable cerebral organization, one which is particularly sensitive to the effects of stress.

The view currently held by most neurologists is that both ambilaterality and dyslexia are the expressions of a common factor, namely immaturity of cerebral development. Gooddy and Reinhold (1961), who also support the hypothesis of maturational lag, have expressed themselves in somewhat different terms. They stressed the idea that in normal circumstances asymmetry of the functions of the two cerebral hemispheres is established as a child develops, and that this asymmetry of function is closely related to the performance of reading and writing. Children with developmental dyslexia, however, fail to establish such an asymmetry of function in the cerebral hemispheres.

Why only a proportion of ill-lateralized children should be dyslexic is not easy to understand. Some psychologists have in the past been reluctant to accept any conception of sinistrality, or of mixed or inadequate dominance, in the context of dyslexia. Gates and Bond (1936) objected that eye and hand dominance have little to do with reading-difficulties. Somewhat similar views were put forward by Woody and Phillips (1934); Gates and Bond (1936); Kirk, Teegarden, Witty and Kopel (1936); Wolfe (1941), and others. Vernon (1957) could not understand how incomplete lateralization and general lack of maturation could explain an inability to learn to read, and therefore she was

* The factor of brilliance does not influence the subject's choice of starting-point, as I have been able to demonstrate by inverting the board, so that the dark colour rather than the light is on the extreme left.

reluctant to accept the evidence. This is not logical. Theories which attributed reading-disability to some general lack of maturation were, to her, unsatisfactory, in that they gave no explanation as to why reading alone should be affected, and not other cognitive activities. She would have expected some general retardation, or at least slow development of all language-faculties, were the defect due to lack of maturation. However, she went on to admit that lack of maturation might be a predisposing factor, some other process being necessary in order to precipitate the disability. Furthermore, she conceded that there might exist a class of individuals who are diffusely retarded in maturation, who exhibit no well-established laterality, and who show disorders of speech and motility, temperamental instability and reading-disability. Such a condition may be hereditary. Vernon gave details of two such examples and went on to say, "clearly such cases form a small minority of all the cases of reading-disability".

This isolation of an immaturity syndrome is, of course, very reminiscent of what Eustis had described ten years earlier. Out of a pedigree comprising 33 descendants, 14 displayed one or more features of a "syndrome" comprising speech-delay or defect; left-handedness or ambidexterity; clumsiness; and also specific reading-disability. Eustis looked upon this syndrome as representing a rather specialized lag in development, and he spoke of a slow tempo of neuro-muscular maturation, probably the result of delayed myelination of motor and associational nerve-tracts.

Undoubtedly, however, some dyslexics are unequivocal dextrals with no family history of left-handedness or ambidexterity. In the absence of any closer correlation it is therefore tempting to invoke a hypothesis which would seek to attribute dyslexia to an underlying delayed, or incomplete, lateralization of certain cerebral functions. Zangwill (1962) wondered whether there might be two sorts of developmental dyslexia, namely a type occurring in poorly lateralized individuals, as opposed to a type presenting in individuals who are lateralized fully. He had been struck by the frequent association of retarded speech-development, defects of spatial perception, motor clumsiness and other indications of defective maturation in cases of dyslexia presenting in ill-lateralized or else left-handed children. Moreover, Zangwill was impressed by the comparative "purity" of the dyslexia when it presents itself in unequivocally right-handed children, and he suggested that a specific genetical factor might plausibly be assumed in this particular group.

The relationship between types of cerebral dominance and the occurrence of dyslexia is obviously a subject which is complicated by two factors which have not yet been completely clarified in the literature. In the first place the question of cerebral dominance is a much more complex matter than has been assumed in the past, as we have already emphasized. That is to say a child may be only "relatively" right-handed or left-handed, as judged by the analysis of a formula of manual skills and postures. The second point is the fact that in correlating handedness with dyslexia it has often been only too obvious that some authors have been using a material made up of diverse types of poor reading ability, not all of which were true cases of developmental dyslexia.

Realizing that only some ill-lateralized children have reading-problems Zangwill put forward three tentative explanations. The first possible idea is that poorly developed laterality and reading-defect could both be due to the effects of an actual cerebral lesion. A second hypothesis is that the reading-difficulty and the lack of cerebral asymmetry could both be taken as evidence of a constitutional maturational lag. The third possibility—and this is the one which Zangwill seemed cautiously to favour—is that the children who lack firm lateral preferences happen also to be particularly vulnerable to the effects of stress—though how this situation conduces to dyslexia was not pursued.

Chapter IX
Minor neurological signs

Cases of "specific" or developmental dyslexia are not always entirely "pure" in the sense of a disability existing in complete isolation. This statement in no way detracts from the neurological conception of developmental dyslexia as a specific constitutional genetically determined defect lying within the middle zone of a spectrum of non-specific reading disorders. The occasional "impurity" of the syndrome is shown by the elucidation *at times*, on appropriate testing, of various subtle, tenuous, or miniscule deficits, or "soft" neurological signs—to employ an unfortunate term. Some of these are virtually "minimal" and may elude superficial examination, coming to light only after more searching techniques. Many of these little signs are related to an incomplete maturation of the nervous system, and they are more likely to be found among the younger age-groups, being rarer in dyslexics who have attained adolescence. This is well shown by the battery of tests used by de Hirsch for the prediction of dyslexics between the ages of $5\frac{1}{2}$ to $6\frac{1}{2}$ years.

The principal deficits which may be brought to light on appropriate testing by what has been called an "extended" or "expanded" neurological examination, include the following: (1) disorders of spatial thought; (2) impaired temporal notions; (3) inadequate, inconsistent, or mixed cerebral dominance; (4) defects of speech or of language, other than dyslexia; (5) disorders of motility; and (6) poor figure-background discrimination.

At the same time, it appears necessary to emphasize strongly that no cluster or combination of defects exists, which can be looked upon as pathognomonic, or as constituting a diagnostic formula. This error is often made by critics.

Disorders of spatial thought and spatial manipulation are important even though demonstrable only in the minority of cases.

The statement made by Gooddy and Reinhold (1961) that there is invariably a right-left disorientation of some degree goes too far. German writers have referred to a *Labilität der Raumlage* (instability of spatial notions) in this setting. When spatial disabilities occur, they recall those met with in adult patients with parietal lobe lesions, differing however in that they are manifesting themselves at an earlier age, and that they are less elaborate and less conspicuous. As in acquired parietal disease they are highly diverse in their nature.

Spatial disabilities may sometimes be displayed in the spontaneous drawings executed by dyslexics. Often there is a conspicuous lack of perspective in, say, pictures of a house. Or there may be a dimensional

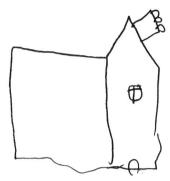

Fig. 41 Spontaneous drawing of a house executed by a left-handed boy of 5 years and 7 months, with a family history of dyslexia. The direction of automatic gaze ran from right to left. A drawing of a man rated at 5¾ years according to the Goodenough scale. In his attempts to write, the child rotated letters and reversed groups of letters. He was regarded as a probable "pre-dyslexic".

confusion so that elevation and plan are jumbled up in an odd manner. Even greater spatial defects may at times be shown when the dyslexic draws from memory a clock-face or a bicycle. Their efforts may be unco-ordinated and even confused. Still greater difficulty is encountered when the child tries to model with plasticine and to construct simple three-dimensional figures or shapes. The dyslexic child may mix up extra-corporeal spatial directions such as up and down, and more often still, left and right. Prepositions such as "on", "under", "below", "behind", "beyond" may be muddled. In attempting to write or to make arithmetical calculations, the child may set down the words and figures upon the paper in an irregular and even haphazard fashion. Figures and words are not placed under each other in correct alignment: the left-hand margins may be too narrow or too wide, and often they descend obliquely. When executing a drawing many children make an unexpectedly small sketch, and position it in the top left or right hand corner rather than boldly in the centre of a blank sheet of paper. (See Fig. 42.)

More severe manifestations of spatial impairment, typical of a parietal lesion in the adult, are rare in dyslexics.

A variant of spatial disorientation is the phenomenon of confusion between right and left in ordinary semi-automatic activities. Though this is not wholly unknown in normal subjects it is certainly more often encountered in those who are backward in reading. Ordinarily this is conspicuous in the younger age-group, and as the dyslexic becomes older, he may outgrow this difficulty. A dyslexic with right-left confusion may rely upon a scar on a finger, which indicates sidedness to him. One boy in my series would always orientate himself spatially by first closing the left eyelid, being unable to wink with the right. The

Fig. 42 Drawing of a man.

Male patient aged 8 years with reading and spelling ages of less than 6 years. I.Q. "average". The drawing rates at a 6-year level according to the Goodenough scale. Crossed lateral. Slow at constructional tasks. Automatic ocular gaze proceeded from right to left. Family history of inaccurate spelling.

confusion in lateral dimensions in the adult may pass unnoticed until special circumstances bring it into the open. Thus when the poor reader is drafted into the Armed Forces he may mix up his right and his left in the barrack square to a degree which transcends the usual awkwardness of a recruit. In the Royal Navy the new entry may muddle up port and starboard. According to Hermann an officer in the Danish army observed that recruits who had been selected for special coaching because of illiteracy, were also those who had been notorious for their right-left confusion at squad drill. Hermann also referred to the case of a taxi-driver in Copenhagen who was so word-blind that he could not cope with his book-work, and who was also hopelessly inept at distinguishing right from left. To surmount this latter defect he was in the habit of putting a black chalk mark on the right thumbnail before attending to a passenger's instructions to turn this way or that.

More banal disorders entailing both motility and spatial notions are seen in those dyslexics who are poor at ball-games; who cannot catch a ball in flight; or who take an unconscionable time to learn to ride a bicycle or a scooter. One must stress firmly however that such dyslexics are in the great minority. Most of the children I have examined have been at least of average attainment: many indeed have excelled in sport, especially swimming and pony-riding. All have been keen cyclists and most seemed to have learned this art with surprising celerity. Oddly enough some dyslexic children in my series have been relatively skilful in chess-playing. Constructional tasks which embrace spatial concepts include the copying of three-dimensional models made with bricks, and also the assembling of jig-saw puzzles, a game which may not be easy for some of these dyslexics. This difficulty is readily assessed by the test of Kohs' blocks, where a few dyslexics fare

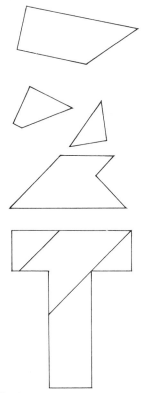

Fig. 43 A particularly difficult assembly-puzzle, which baffles most youngsters, in that it represents a high-level test of a spatio-constructional character.

badly. Again, such difficulties are encountered in only the minority.

Spatio-constructional difficulties can also be demonstrated in some cases by simple formboard tests (see Figs. 45 and 46). In such circumstances a few dyslexic children are slow and hesitating in their execution, and may indeed even fail to complete the task. The examiner should surreptitiously time with a stop-watch the child's performance, and make a note on the record.

Fig. 44 A coloured picture has been cut into nine pieces, and the assemblage of these parts represents a simple test for constructional ability.

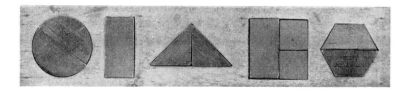

Fig. 45 A simple form-board test of spatio-constructional ability. The triangular figure in the centre presents the principal difficulty.

Fig. 46 Sponge rubber inset puzzle, used to investigate spatio-constructional skill. This test is more difficult than the assembling of the form-board shown in Fig. 45. Anything less than two minutes as the time taken to complete this task, may be regarded as "excellent".

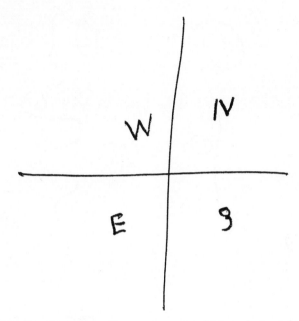

Fig. 47 Drawing of a compass. Shown a cross, the child was instructed to indicate north, south, east and west.

Tjossem *et al.* found that reversals and rotations were common with a simple "reversible figures test" up to the age of $8\frac{1}{2}$ years in slow readers, the mean rotational score being 3·4. Over the age of $8\frac{1}{2}$, however, this kind of defect was less common, the mean rotational score being now only 0·4. The tendency to reversals and rotations of symbols was more pronounced within the population of slow readers, the tendency diminishing, however, with age. On the other hand the visual retention test of Benton is usually performed quite well, and without mirror-opposite errors.

Dyslexic children can usually copy with accuracy a meaningless scribble, thus showing no constructional apraxia. However if the model is deliberately constituted so as to entail a series of loops, some to the right and some to the left, the dyslexic may become confused. In his copy he may draw right-hand curlicues instead of left, or *vice versa*. (See Fig. 48).

Closely bound up with disorders of spatial though in dyslexics, are the evidences of inadequate temporal notions. Some dyslexics show an imperfect sense of rhythm. Ideas of "sequence" are of particular importance in that they combine conceptions which are of both a spatial and temporal nature. According to Vernon, some dyslexics find difficulty in matching visual patterns with auditory rhythms (as in

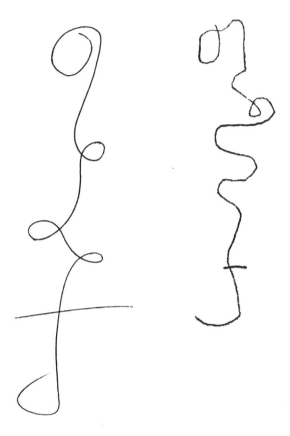

Fig. 48 Test for constructional apraxia. The boy was instructed to copy the model on the left. Note the reversal of one loop and the omission of others. The subject was 11 years of age, with reading and spelling ages of little over 6. He was slow in the execution of spatio-constructional tasks, and he was confused as to right-left dimensions. There was a positive family history of reading retardation and spelling defects.

Stambak's test), though able to reproduce either of these individually. Sequential disorders are of extreme importance in dyslexics for they may conceivably point to the fundamental nature of the underlying defect. There are some who cannot recite in correct serial order the days of the week or months of the year, and who confuse the time-incidence of important occasions in history. Memory of past events may not be well organized, and one child could not indicate in correct sequence the outstanding events which had happened to her. Failure to enumerate correctly the calendar months was specially noted by Engler, and by Laubenthal. Bender also stressed these temporal defects, and in her series of dyslexic children she found some who muddled past, present and future, and who could not understand the various tenses of the verbs. Terms such as "now", "then", "tomorrow", "yesterday" had but little meaning for them. To some of her children the phrase "the first day of the week" conveyed very little, for they saw no more reason for starting on the left-hand side of the calendar with a Sunday, than on the right with a Saturday.

Learning to tell the time is a delayed accomplishment in most dyslexics. Thus in my series of dyslexics 100 were late in learning to read a clock, 6 years being assumed as the usual age for a normal child. One youngster asked why it was that the long hand of the clock was for the minutes and the short hand for the hours, when hours were so much longer than minutes.

Sequential difficulties of these kinds are not too uncommon, and they may account for some of the disorders of spelling made by the older dyslexics. At a later age, after some competency in reading has been achieved, difficulties in spelling ordinarily continue. Such "ex-dyslexics" typically find it anything but an easy task to consult a dictionary or a telephone directory, as already stated.

In later life the dyslexic may also experience considerable difficulty in learning the Morse system of signalling. Indeed, it was this particular disability which brought a Royal Naval Cadet to my notice during the war (Critchley, 1942), who in all probability was an ex-dyslexic. This case reminds us of Vernon's observation that dyslexics often cannot match visuo-auditory rhythms.

Certain authors, and especially those who have associated developmental dyslexia with a global retardation in the acquisition of language, have drawn attention to the co-existence of disorders of articulate speech in dyslexic children. Some have emphasized a comparatively late age at which the child uttered its first word, or strung together words in logical fashion to form phrases or sentences. An immature or dyslalic disorder of speaking has often been observed though usually it proves to be merely a transient phenomenon. Thus disorders of articulation or of the development of articulate speech were reported in 30% of the cases observed by Kågen (1943); 41% of the boys and 32% of the girls in the dyslexics studied by Hallgren (1952); in certain of Ingram's cases (1959); and in 16 out of the 23 dyslexics described by Hibbert (1961). In my series of 125 children presented with reading or spelling problems, 41 had been late in the acquisition of speech. Besides late development of speech, and imperfections in articulation, there may also be demonstrable at times an immaturity of the faculty of *language* as opposed to speech. Thus inadequacies in syntax and in vocabulary may at times be discerned. For example, the child may emit what might be called reversals of concepts, saying, for example, black for white, nice for nasty. In my experience this has been most exceptional. Direction is frequently muddled but it is often hard to decide whether it is a spatial or a linguistic defect. Saunders referred to reversals of time-sequences, whereby the dyslexic child may say first for last, now for later, seldom for often. One child within his series said "the day after yesterday . . . I mean the day before tomorrow", when what he really meant was the day after tomorrow (1962). However, these disorders of language and of diction are inconsistent, and they are best regarded as being epiphenomena, and rare at that.

Reference has already been made to a difficulty occasionally met with in dyslexics, in retailing back in his own words a story which has been told to him. Some parents have said that their dyslexic child experiences great awkwardness in expressing himself verbally—stammering and stuttering, and finding himself at a loss for the appropriate words in which to clothe his thought. Other parents have reported differently, stating that their child can emit his ideas well enough in articulate speech, but that he falls down completely when it comes to written work.

Such observations are of extreme interest, for they may be taken as suggestive of a high-level disorder of cognition. Alternatively, of course, a more peripheral defect may be operative, namely a cluttering in the former case, and a severe writing disability in the latter.

But the explanation of semantic and syntactical disorders of self-expression may be simpler. A dyslexic reaches adolescence with an inadequate vocabulary, unless extreme efforts have been made at compensation along auditory channels. The adult dyslexic is only too often lame in his manipulation of language-symbols.

Faust has claimed to have identified two curious defects in association with developmental dyslexia, and which suggest something in the nature of visual dysgnosia. In the first place he found an odd inability on the part of a dyslexic to interpret the meaning of people's facial expressions, especially when depicted in pictorial form. Secondly, he observed a simultanagnosia, that is, an inability to grasp the meaning of a picture as a whole. These claims are unfortunate, in that they suggest an experience with secondary cases of reading-retardation. In my series of dyslexics these two observations of Faust have certainly never been confirmed. Interpretation of both facial expressions and of representational pictures has been strikingly accurate and even shrewd.

Yet another complicated visual defect in dyslexics—which has already been mentioned—is a difficulty in distinguishing colours and also in naming them correctly, as specifically reported by Warburg. However, a defect in colour-naming has not been found in any of my cases. In my series, minor defects of colour vision demonstrated by some of the isochromatic charts in the Ishihara test, have come to light a few times, an incidence which is probably non-significant.

Among the motility-disorders which can at times be discerned in dyslexic children is a general *gaucherie* or awkwardness. The gait may be shambling. The child may run in an ungainly fashion, and frequently tumble. Manual dexterity may be so maladroit as to raise the suspicion of a "congenital" type of motor dyspraxia. Because of muscular inco-ordination the dyslexic child may find it hard to bounce a ball, to tie and untie knots, or to fasten and unfasten buttons. These shortcomings were particularly stressed by Rabinovitch (1954) who wrote, "observation of gait, and the performance of motor acts such as dressing, opening and closing doors, and the handling of psychological test-materials, led to the definite impression of a non-specific awkwardness and clumsiness in motor function".

Again I would stress that inordinate clumsiness is anything but an invariable symptom. Indeed it is rare. Of my series of 125 cases, it was noted in 34. When present it was more commonly encountered in the very young dyslexics. Most of my patients actually showed real dexterity. Some of them excelled at model-making and other mechanical pursuits. Among the little girls, there were not a few who gave promise at ballet dancing classes.

However, in "symptomatic" cases of dyslexia, where underlying brain-damage appears to be a likely factor, manual and digital awkwardness is common. During the performance of routine neurological testing for dexterity, the patient may also be observed to make unconscious small-range synkinetic mirror-movements with the opposite hand: or else to make more diffuse squirming or grimacing movements involving the face, trunk and limbs in an uninhibited fashion.

Bender has repeatedly drawn attention to the persistence of a tonic neck reflex in lateral deviation of the outstretched hands, a phenomenon which normally disappears at the age of $6\frac{1}{2}$ to $7\frac{1}{2}$ years. I have rarely found this in a dyslexic over the age of 8 years.

When the Bender Gestalt battery of tests is put to dyslexic children, several complicated motor-spatio-constructional defects may be uncovered. The following have been described; (1) figures which appear primitive, "fluid" and full of movement of the vertical, whirling type; (2) "rounding" of squared figures; replacement of dots by loops; squaring off of diamond shapes; obliquity or tilting of vertical or horizontal lines; (3) some disorientation of the background, usually by rotation of mobile figures, or by "verticalization"; (4) closure of open figures; and (5) a tendency for the child to convert figures, especially those that are verticalized and closed, into a man, by drawing a face within the enclosure. Lachmann (1960) found in dyslexics a five-fold type of distortion, viz. angulation, rotation, primitivation, separation and slant. The presence of these anomalies, especially in the younger age-groups, readily distinguished children with reading-disabilities from normal subjects. But quite often emotionally disturbed good readers also showed these same distortions. Other authors had previously noted some of these phenomena (e.g. rotation by Fabian, 1945; angulation by Silver, 1953; and primitivation by de Hirsch, 1954).

It has already been stated that some dyslexics, though certainly not all, may fare badly at arithmetic. Apart from a slowness in identifying numerical symbols, there may be an incapacity to grasp ideas of number and relative size. A difficulty in learning and retaining multiplication tables may be present. The principles underlying addition, subtraction, multiplication and division may never be mastered, constituting a veritable "developmental dyscalculia"—whatever is implied by that ill-understood entity. Again there are two other interesting and not unrelated disabilities which have already been referred to, namely a disorientation in lateral dimension, and a finger-agnosia. Immediately one is reminded of what used to be spoken of as a Gerstmann's syndrome, with its four cardinal components of dysgraphia, dyscalculia, right-left disorientation and finger-agnosia, consequent upon a lesion of the dominant parietal lobe. Could dyslexia therefore be a manifestation of an inherent Gerstmann's syndrome, as was originally suggested by Hermann and Norrie?

Both dyslexia and Gerstmann's syndrome have been ascribed by some to a common factor of directional dysfunction, the result of a failure of lateral orientation with reference to corporeal awareness, and the organization of self within extra-personal space. However important, this point can scarcely be fundamental, for a Gerstmann syndrome is certainly not an integral part of dyslexia, even though right-left confusion is commoner in dyslexics than in normal readers, but perhaps only to a slight degree. Benton and Kemble (1960) believed that dyslexics show only a mild tendency towards a malperformance of higher order right-left orientation-exercises. This they interpreted as a reflection of a relative impairment in symbolization and conceptualization. One other alleged component of a Gerstmann's syndrome is finger-agnosia. Although some writers have drawn attention to finger-agnosia among dyslexic children, the notion should be viewed most critically. The gallimaufry of "tests" have the principal effect of bewildering both testor and testee, and are, in my opinion, not worth the time expended. Neurologists today realize that the unfortunate term "finger-agnosia" means different things to different writers, and the term probably does not represent any true clinical entity. Benton is strongly critical of the validity of Gerstmann's syndrome. Similar doubts have also been ventilated by other writers, e.g. Heimburger, Demyer and Reitan (1964), Critchley (1966), and Poeck and Orgass (1967). The propriety of thinking in terms of a "constitutional" or "congenital" variety is even more suspect. I express this opinion advisedly having been responsible in 1942 for the reporting of what has often been regarded as the first recorded case of a congenital Gerstmann syndrome. As I declared in my Gowers Memorial Lecture

(1965), this publication was in that respect unfortunate, and went on to say "... If then I am unconvinced as to the *bona fides* of Gerstmann's syndrome, I am even more dubious of the doctrine of a developmental variety. I plead guilty to having been in 1942 one of the begetters of this heresy, but there is no enormity in a change of opinion. Like Winston Churchill ... 'my views are a harmonious process, which keeps them in relation to the current movement of events'."

Money has stressed the confusion between visual images and the body-scheme which seems to underlie the difficulties of directional orientation in dyslexics. Their problem is not just a simple one of right-left confusion, nor yet one of difficulty with perception of form in two dimensions. "It is truly a three-dimensional *space-movement* perception problem, involving the relationship of the visual image to the body image ahead and behind, toward and away-from, left and right, and facing upward or downward".

In concluding an account of the minor neurological signs which may at times be demonstrated in dyslexics, reference may be made to the occurrence of high-level sensory disturbances, as described by Rabinovitch *et al.* These authors found delay in the appreciation of double face-hand tactile stimuli; inaccurate localization of touch; and impaired two-point discrimination.

In recapitulating the diverse neurological disorders which may be uncovered after close and particular scrutiny, it must be stressed that *these findings are by no means integral. Many a dyslexic—perhaps even most of them—shows no such disabilities despite highly alerted and scrupulous testing-procedures. Perhaps these subtle neurological signs should be regarded as epiphenomena—significant when they occur, but not essential in any consideration as to pathogenesis or aetiology. When such manifestations are found, there seems to be an inverse correlation with the age of the patient. In other words, the younger the subject the more likely it is that neurological signs will be found, while with older dyslexics the greater the likelihood of a negative clinical examination. When neurological disabilities are marked, or when they persist into late childhood, underlying brain-damage is probable. The dyslexia would then be of the "symptomatic" or "secondary" kind.*

Some authors have tried to isolate certain neurological groupings and to relate them in a causal fashion with the occurrence of dyslexia. We have already referred to the Hermann-Norrie conception of a developmental Gerstmann syndrome. Silver and Hagin (1960) were able to demonstrate in 92% of their cases a syndrome comprising: (1) visuo-motor immaturity; (2) specific difficulty in spatial orientation (angulation difficulties; confusion in figure-background perception); (3) inability to grasp the temporal relationships of sounds; and (4) body-image distortion, with "tonus and postural problems".

The neurological conspectus of developmental dyslexia includes the evidence of electro-encephalography. Its diagnostic role is admittedly minor in character. Mild dysrhythmias are often found, suggestive of cortical immaturity, and these may be most evident in the parieto-occipital areas bilaterally.

Even more interesting electrophysiological observations in dyslexics have also been made. Tuller and Eames (1966) studied 7 children who were poor readers; all showed deviations in the parietal and posterior temporal regions which correlated fairly well with the degree of reading-retardation. No single or specific type of dysrhythmia could be isolated. Baro (1966) referred to electro-encephalographic abnormalities which were precipitated in poor readers by dint of the act of trying to read. Oettinger (1964) studied 26 dyslexic patients and found that in 8 instances electro-encephalographic abnormalities were induced by the act of reading and he spoke in this connection of "sub-clinical reading epilepsy". In 15 out of the 26 there was an increase in muscle-spiking which began in the cervical and temporal regions and often spread. Oettinger, Nekonski and Gill (1967) found a dysrhythmia provoked by reading in 5 out of 19 patients with reading problems. One of these developed an autonomic seizure while reading, and another later developed grand mal while watching television. In a personally observed relatively small series of dyslexics studied electro-encephalographically by Cobb* and in another group by Pampiglione†, no convincing case was found which could be regarded as an instance of subclinical reflex reading epilepsy.

An electro-encephalographic study of 157 dyslexics has been made by Hughes and Park (1968). Abnormal records were found in 56 cases (35·6%), the majority being "mild" in nature. The most common type of electrical abnormality was the 6–7 and 14-sec. positive spike phenomenon. The weakness of this particular investigation concerns the diagnostic standards of dyslexia. The full scale I.Q. was reduced as low as 85; and the difference between reading and chronological ages was as little as 1·5 years. Although various ophthalmological tests were carried out as well as a neutrophil determination, nothing was mentioned as regards the clinico-neurological findings. To date therefore it would seem that the electro-encephalogram provides very little in the way of diagnostic assistance.

All the foregoing clinical findings in dyslexics necessarily differ according to the age of the subject. As already mentioned, neurological anomalies are likely to be more conspicuous in dyslexics of the younger age-group. In adult dyslexics diagnosis is relatively easier provided one can gauge and allow for possible psychiatric overlays. The problem is more difficult in very young children, where cases of true specific dyslexia have to be identified and distinguished from children who are

*Personal communication.
†Personal communication.

backward in learning to read for other reasons, such as general intellectual retardation. The series of tests described by de Hirsch is
therefore a useful guide to diagnosis. She asserted that at the early age
of $5\frac{1}{2}$ years the putative dyslexics often show themselves to be fidgety
children, a feature which had been independently noted by Creak.
Their movements are jerky and clumsy. Isolated skilled actions may be
marred by global motor responses. Their spontaneous drawings may
be revealing.

In a detailed study, de Hirsch, Jansky and Langford (1962–1965) *de Hirsch*
employed a battery of 37 perceptuo-motor and linguistic tests to a
series made up of 53 children together with another 53 who had been
born prematurely. Of these tests 10 were found to be valuable as
constituting a "predictive index". Certain pre-school children could be
isolated on the basis of these defects as "high risk" subjects from the
standpoint of subsequent difficulties with reading and with spelling.
The ten tests which between them afforded a 91 % correlation were the
following:

1. *Pencil use* or *mastery*, as determined by the child's skill in
   grasping and controlling the implement.
2. *Bender's visuo-motor Gestalt Test* with special reference to the
   response to the essentials of the Gestalt; the degree of differentiation; and the ability to organize the figures in space.
3. *Wepman's auditory discrimination Test*, using 20 pairs of words.
4. *Number of words* employed during story-telling ("The Three
   Bears").
5. *Categories.* The child's ability to produce generic names for
   three clusters of words, as reflecting his ability to categorize.
6. *Horst reversals test* (part 2) in which the child is required to
   match letter-sequences.
7. *Gates' word-matching and rhyming test* (abbreviated).
8. *Word-recognition* (1). The child is taught two words, e.g.
   "boy" and "train". Two hours later he is expected to pick out
   these two words from a series of cards presented successively.
9. *Word-recognition* (2). The child is expected to pick out after
   2 hours the words "boy" and "train" from a collection of 10
   cards exposed simultaneously upon a table.

and 10. *Word reproduction.* After 2 hours the child must write from
   memory as much of the two words "boy" and "train" as he
   could recall.*

Comparing the after-histories of the children born at term with
those that were premature, de Hirsch *et al.* found that the academic

*High-level scores for the foregoing were as follows: (1) level of competence
expected for age; (2) 5 out of 6; (3) 14 out of 15; (4) 226 words or more; (5) 3 (of 3)
correctly named; (6) at least 5 out of 9; (7) 9 out of 12; (8) the finding of both words;
(9) both words; (10) 3 out of 6.

performance of the latter was still inferior to that of the former even at the end of the second grade. Such children were considered as falling into an academic "risk" group. Other features mentioned by the authors as being common among those destined to become poor readers were: small stature; hyperactivity; distractability; impulsiveness; lack of inhibition; occasionally hypoactivity; ready fatigue; babyish behaviour; and short span of auditory memory. Some of these features should, I suggest, be accepted with reserve.

Prediction of dyslexia has also been carried out in Belgium by Limbosch, Luminet-Jasinski, and Dierkens-Dopchie (1968), upon a series of children attending primary and nursery schools (*jardins des enfants*). Their battery of tests included Goodenough's draw-a-man; visual recall of differently orientated shapes (Borel-Maisonny); copying of a complex geometrical figure (*la Goutte*); reproduction of visuo-auditory rhythms (Stambak); a rapid articulatory test; Kohs' blocks; a vocabulary test; and right-left discrimination.

Detailed psycho-motor profiles have been given of a very young dyslexic by Jansky (1958), and of an adult dyslexic by Pflugfelder (1948). It would be dangerously easy however to be misled by single case-reports which are quite exceptional in character. Pflugfelder's patient is interesting in that his strong eidetic imagery seems to run counter to what other writers upon dyslexia have claimed. In the Johns Hopkins symposium upon Dyslexia (1961) it was suggested that the dyslexic was one who had difficulty not only in establishing the necessary lexical concepts, visual and auditory, and in relating the visual and phonic images, but was also in some way a non-visile cognitional type. As Money said, the dyslexic is perhaps weak in visual imagery and visual memory of all types, quite unlike one who is endowed with eidetic imagery and a photographic memory.

Chapter X
Genetic properties

We owe to genetics the most cogent single argument in support of the conception of a constitutional specific type of dyslexia identifiable among the miscellany of cases of poor readers. Although as long ago as 1905 it was observed that congenital word-blindness might involve more than one member of a family, this aspect attracted little notice at first. The pioneer here was Thomas who found six patients within two generations of a single family. In the same year Herbert Fisher recorded congenital word-blindness in an uncle and a nephew. The following year Stephenson went so far as to postulate a recessive mode of inheritance on the basis of six cases cropping up in three generations. Hinshelwood and also McCready observed a familial occurrence. Plate (1910) found poor readers among three generations, as did Rønne (1936) and also Marshall and Ferguson (1939). In 1911 Warburg ventured the opinion that dyslexia was often transmitted by the unaffected mother. He also stressed the important point that the information supplied by a parent is not always wholly reliable, for there is a common tendency to "play down" a familial incidence. Illing (1929), who found hereditary factors in seven out of eleven cases, discovered that in three of his patients both parents were poor readers. Laubenthal (1936) published a complicated pedigree in which dyslexia was associated with many examples of mental defect, criminal propensity, and psychopathy; he asserted that in severe cases of word-blindness it was justifiable to carry out sterilization. This publication, be it noted, emanated from Nazi Germany.

Scandinavian researchers in particular have afforded valuable evidence as to the importance of genetic factors in dyslexia. Norrie (1939) found familial tendencies in "practically all" of her cases. Kågen (1943) mentioned hereditary properties in 30%, and Ramer (1947) in 50 to 60% of their dyslexics. Skydsgaard published a number of pedigrees which obviously revealed a genetical factor, though of uncertain nature. Most important has been the monograph of Hallgren (1950) based upon 276 cases, all but six being personally observed. In his experience 88% of all cases had reading problems in one or more relatives. The cases were made up of children attending the Stockholm Child Guidance Clinic, together with others from either a *Folkskola* or a *Larsverk*, i.e. elementary or secondary schools; Hallgren divided his material into four groups in the following manner: *Group 1*. Families with "secondary cases" (i.e. proband's sibs and *both* parents affected with specific dyslexia) (3 probands and 8 secondary cases); *Group 2*. Families with secondary cases and *one* parent affected (94 probands

and 147 secondary cases); *Group 3*. Families with both parents unaffected and cases of specific dyslexia among the proband's sibs, sibs
of their parents, or grandparents of the probands (7 probands and 5
secondary cases); and *Group 4*. Solitary cases (12). The author concluded
that developmental dyslexia follows a monohybrid autosomal dominant
mode of inheritance. Furthermore Hallgren, and also Norrie, made
studies upon twins with dyslexia. The total number of pairs investigated
was 45, of which 12 were monozygotic and 33 dizygotic. There was a
100% concordance in the former group, as opposed to 33% in the
latter. Other instances of dyslexia among identical twins have been
described by Brander (1935), Ley and Tordeur (1936), Jenkins, Brown
and Elmendorf (1937), and by Schiller (1937).

Mattlinger (1941) also studied the family histories in her total series
of 285. She found distinct evidence of dyslexia among the relatives in
95 cases (i.e. 33·4%), and probable evidence in another 49 cases (or
17·2%). This indicated that one dyslexic child in two probably had a
positive family history. Eliminating those case-histories where the
information was imprecise, the figures rose to 50·8% and 26·2%,
giving a total of 77%.

Vernon adopted a rather critical attitude towards the genetic factor
in cases of retarded reading, and sceptical of the existence of a specific
form of dyslexia, she found it difficult to accept Hallgren's conclusion
that specific reading disability is in most cases a single and isolated
congenital entity. She required further corroborative evidence
from other studies, despite the minute care and skill with which
Hallgren assembled and analyzed his material. Vernon thought it
more plausible to assert that there is a congenital disposition in certain
cases towards the occurrence of various related defects; reading disability; speech-defects or infantile speech; motor inco-ordination;
left-handedness or ambidexterity. But, seven years before, Hallgren had
expressly examined and unequivocally stated that his present study
lent no support to the hypothesis that specific dyslexia, mental deficiency, nervous disorders, left-handedness and speech-defects were
different phenotypical manifestations of the same hereditary taint.

Rutter (1968) has also attempted to discount the genetical factor,
suggesting that in his experience the "family history in part reflected a
social inheritance rather than a biological transmission".

These criticisms strike one as belonging to the category of special
pleading, if not sheer shadow-boxing. To anyone experienced in clinical
diagnosis, it seems impossible to overlook the very real heredo-familial
incidence in cases of specific developmental dyslexia.

It has almost always been observed that developmental dyslexia
affects males more often than females. Jastak alone could find no sex
difference in his series (1934). The estimate varies from one author to
another. The table on page 91 illustrates the reported sex-incidence as

determined by a number of authors. Of my own 616 cases referred to me as potential dyslexics, and personally examined, 487 were males and 129 were females.

We can therefore assume that about 4 males to 1 female may be accepted as a reasonable figure.

Again, Vernon is out of concord on the question of sex-incidence. She believed that the claimed preponderance of boys was because boys who are non-readers create more trouble at school than girls; or at least they bring their disability more forcibly to the teacher's notice, while girls suffer in silence. This again smacks of special pleading. Perhaps too, according to Vernon, parents take a more serious view of inability to read in a boy than in a girl. However, the explanation which Vernon deemed most likely was that boys with reading disability had superadded emotional disorders, often aggressive in type. Boys are referred to clinics because these latter disorders have brought them to the notice of teachers and parents rather than the disability itself.

Observations such as these, and particularly the last, would not tally with the experience of neurological consultants to whom children with dyslexia are brought by worried parents expressly on account of their paradoxical inability to learn to read. Among such children boys unquestionably outnumber girls.

TABLE III

Author	Year	Percentage of Males	Total No. in series
Bachmann . . .	1927	70	80
Illing . . .	1929	80	12
Anderson and Kelley .	1931	84	100
Monroe . . .	1932	84	50
Brander . . .	1935	100	12
Blanchard . .	1936	86	73
Witty and Kopel	1936	66	100
Creak . . .	1936	76	50
Bennet . . .	1938	72	50
Skydsgaard. . .	1942	80	26
Orton . . .	1943	82	102
Eames . . .	1944	80	100
Wallin . . .	1949	82	120
Norman . . .	1950	76·8	694
Hallgren . . .	1950	76	116
Mattlinger . .	1967	69·8	285
Critchley (1) . .	1967	83·5	115
Critchley (2) . .	1968	79	616
Debray . . .	1968	69	285

But there is yet another odd circumstance which must be reckoned with, even though the explanation be obscure. Paediatricians have not infrequently found in their hospitals a higher incidence in boys than girls of a medley of disorders, not all of them learning-disabilities. This applies for example to such acquired conditions as meningitis, though it might conceivably be adduced in explanation that among young children, boys were at greater risk.

The question may be discussed whether the position of the dyslexic child within the birth-series is important. Warburg, it will be recalled, invoked the notion of maternal *Produktionserschöpfung* and he had the idea that dyslexia was most likely to occur in the youngest member of a large family. His conclusions were based upon the small series of 21 families. This was in 1911. But considerations other than purely genetic ones may possibly be all-important. Twenty years later Anderson and Kelley, dealing with a group of 100 cases of reading disability, found a significantly smaller number of solitary children or of eldest children, affected with dyslexia. They believed that parental solicitude was more likely to be operative in the case of an only child who was backward in reading, or in a first child. Bennet (1938) found a smaller number of eldest children (8 out of 50) affected with dyslexia as compared with a control group of 17 out of 50 where the first-born was not affected. Hallgren (1950) went into the problem of ordinal position much more carefully than previous authors. He found that children with dyslexia are distributed among the different numbers in the birth-series, and considered that position in birth-series could not be a causal factor of importance in specific dyslexia. Thus, out of his Clinic material 55·5 cases were found in the first half of the sibship and 72·5 among the second half. The corresponding figures for the school material were 29·5 and 33·5, and for the two groups together, 79·5 and 100·5. The differences were not regarded as significant. If only the sibs of probands are included, 37·5 cases were found in the first half of the sibship, and 33·5 in the second.

Harris (1961), investigating the factor of birth-order in children with learning difficulties, found that youngest or last-born children were twice as often affected. The author related this difference to the factor of parental ambitions. In the series of 20 cases followed up by Rawson (1968) 5 were only children; 8 were the oldest of 2 or more; 3 were the middle of 3 or more; and 4 were the youngest of 3 or more.

In my series of 125 random cases (100 boys, 25 girls) the birth-order of the patients with alleged dyslexia is set out in the following table:

	Males (100)	Females (25)
First born	31	6
Second born	39	9
Third born	20	5
Fourth born	5	5
Fifth born	3	—
Adopted	2	—

There were some instances in my total series of 620, where the sibship was complicated by the occurrence of second marriages. Thus a little boy with dyslexia might have an older step-sister: in such cases the patient would be rated as "second born". One such case occurred in my random series of 125.

The above figures can also be broken down by recording whether the first-born was an only child or an eldest (or elder) sib. Thus of the 37 children recorded as being first in ordinal position (31 males, 6 females), 9 were actually the sole offspring, while 28 were to be regarded as the first among a sibship (24 males, 4 females). Similarly the question of whether the dyslexic child is the youngest member of a sibship might be a more important point than the mere numerical place in the family. Thus out of 48 who were noted as being the second born (39 males, 9 females) 29 were actually the younger (22 males, 7 females). Out of those noted as occupying third place (25 cases; 20 males, 5 females), 21 were actually the youngest (17 males, 4 females). Of the fourth born dyslexics (10 cases; 5 males, 5 females) 7 were the youngest (3 boys, 4 girls); while out of the fifth born (3 cases, all males), 2 were the youngest. There were also two adopted boys.

A note as to ordinal position is of limited value without a knowledge of the incidence of multiple sibships within the general population. According to the official figures of the Registrar General for live births in England and Wales during 1967, the distribution was as follows:

Families of one child	303,647
two children	283,622
three ,,	119,025
four ,,	54,073
five ,,	25,486
six or more children	26,333

But figures as to ordinal position are relatively non-significant without data regarding maternal age.

Parental consanguinity was not found to be important in the aetiology of dyslexia in Hallgren's series.

Chapter XI
The size of the problem

Here lies a particularly difficult question. The percentage of dyslexics within the community may well have been overestimated by some writers. Others again have surely played down the magnitude of the problem. Among this latter group belong the very unconvincing figures contained in the Ministry of Education's report on the "Health of the Schoolchild in 1960 and 1961". A few extremists even dispute the very existence of dyslexia. The explanation for the divergence of opinion lies partly in difficulties in clinical diagnosis, but more especially, in the personal prejudices of the observer. The proportion of dyslexics is not the same in different countries, according to some writers. Thus it is often believed that dyslexia is unusually common in the Scandinavian countries. Certainly the disability is well-recognized in that part of the world, specially tested for, and when discovered, appropriately treated. Thus in Denmark, even as long ago as 1951, there were 151 special reading-classes where over 2,500 children attended. This figure did not include the pupils at the Hellerup Word-blind Institute in Copenhagen. Today, in Finland, there are 10 centres where dyslexic children are given instruction, a figure which is additional to the facilities existing within the capital city.

Throughout the world, instances of developmental dyslexia tend to be submerged within the larger population of bad readers, and so their specificity may escape detection. Years ago Nettleship shrewdly asserted that congenital word-blindness was easy to detect in the children of well-educated parents, diagnosis being much more difficult in children who were crowded within our infant elementary schools. The situation even today has not considerably improved.

There is an added problem which crops up when trying to estimate the frequency of dyslexia, namely the necessity to disentangle these specific cases not only from the actual retarded readers, but from out of the general population of educationally deprived individuals. Within this last-named category belong the facultative illiterates, which according to Gray, constitute 50% of the world's population, at least another 15% being "nearly illiterate".

Out of New York's juvenile delinquents in 1955 no fewer than 76% were said to be over 2 years retarded in the Gray's Oral Reading test, and of these over half were retarded by 5 or more years (Harrower). A high percentage has also been found in France, where in Paris out of a population of young offenders between 12 and 16 years of age the proportion of non-readers was said to have been at least 75%. Aside from delinquency, Bauer (1959) opined that eight million retarded readers exist in the United States of America at the present time. According to Rabinovitch *et al.* about 10% of all American children of average intelligence read so badly that their total adjustment is impaired. To what extent these groupings represent a *mélange* of the educationally inadequate, the intellectually deficient, the emotionally disturbed, the infirm of purpose, and the genuine dyslexics, has never been determined. The same uncertainty is attached to figures from England and Wales prepared by the Ministry of Education in 1950, wherein 1·4% of all 15-year-old youngsters were found to be illiterate. By "illiteracy" was understood a reading ability of less than 7 years by the standards of 1938, while a reading ability of between 7 and 8 years was regarded as indicating "semi-illiteracy". This latter group amounted to 4·3%. In each case "silent" reading is implied. The 1956 figures from the Ministry of Education estimated that 15% of all adults belong to the class of illiterates and semi-literates.

Unquestionably official figures from the United Kingdom are wholly unconvincing. The same scepticism applies to the smaller scale surveys that have been carried out in the County of Kent, and also in the Isle of Wight. As regards the latter inquiry, which was confined to school-children aged 9 and 10 years, the prevalence of what was called "specific reading retardation" was 4%.

Reverting to the assessments that have been made by those authors who have dealt specifically with dyslexia, we find that Thomas (1905) guessed that one in every two thousand schoolchildren was con-genitally word-blind. Subsequent authors put the incidence higher. Thus Wallin (1911) found dyslexia in 0·7% of a series of school-children. Hallgren (1950) judged the incidence in Sweden of specific dyslexia within the normal population as roughly 10%, Sinclair (1948), Hermann (1959), Rabinovitch *et al.* (1954) each gauged the occurrence as around 10%. Borel-Maisonny (1951) put the figure as between 3% and 20%. Childs (1959) said 5·5% to 25%; Silver and Hagin (1960) 5% to 25%; and Bender (1957) believed that between 5% and 15% of all schoolchildren were unable to acquire language-skills as rapidly as most youngsters with comparable intellectual ability and schooling. Writing in 1966 Thompson asserted that about 11% of the adult population of the United States had not learned to read up to the fourth-grade level. The Regents' Conference on Improving Reading at the University of the State of New York in 1962 stated that 35% of all American youths were seriously retarded in reading. In the United States, again, the National Institute for Neurological Diseases and Blindness (N.I.N.D.B.) reported (1962) that the prevalence of all forms of reading-disability (as estimated in North America and elsewhere) may be placed at 150 per 1000 schoolchildren, or 15%. With respect to the category commonly called specific dyslexia, 10% is probably a reasonable estimate. Professor Bay, in a personal communication, has estimated the incidence of true specific dyslexia among elementary schoolchildren in Düsseldorf as being between 1 % and 2 %.

The allegedly low incidence of reading-disabilities in Japan deserves comment. Makita's suggestion that it is due to the inherent linguistic merits of the Japanese language is not plausible. The most probable explanation is that in Japan teachers, neurologists and educational psychologists are not alive to the possible occurrence of dyslexia. Should, however, this turn out to be an unfair and incorrect opinion, then it can only be concluded that for genetic reasons the incidence of developmental dyslexia happens to be unusually low in Japan.

Neurologists usually teach that true specific developmental dyslexia (in contrast to non-specific reading-retardation) is a comparatively rare condition, although it must be admitted that there is no scientific evidence available even now as to the precise incidence. Neurologists would agree with Vernon when she asserted that we have no information as to the frequency of congenital reading disability among backward readers in general. She also laid it down that it is unlikely that dyslexics constitute more than a small proportion even of severe cases of reading-disability. Here she is on far less certain grounds. Without doubt, dyslexia is commoner than generally imagined. Cases are constantly being overlooked by teachers, and misinterpreted by educational psychologists, and sometimes even by child psychiatrists. Hermann's figure of 10 % of dyslexics among Danish schoolchildren tallies exactly with Sinclair's survey of primary schools in Edinburgh. Until recently I would have imagined this figure as too high for England, an opinion which was expressed in the first edition of this book in 1964. Today I am less confident, suspecting that the percentage is higher.

Obviously the problem is sufficiently important to merit official recognition. Facilities are sorely needed for the early recognition of dyslexics, followed by opportunities for these children to receive individual, sympathetic, and intensive tuition, either in the classroom or in special schools, residential or otherwise. An even more satisfactory solution would be to train a corps of specialized teachers of dyslexia who could be sent to the schools in sufficient numbers to deal with children who had been screened and later accepted as victims of developmental dyslexia. The problem is one which requires the active participation of neurologists at the diagnostic stage, for differentiation is not always an easy matter.

Chapter XII
Psychiatric repercussions

Reading is a "developmental task"

Developmental dyslexics and indeed all children with difficulty in learning to read, tend quite early to develop neurotic reactions. Sometimes these are severe and may lead to a striking personality change. Nothing could be more natural. Some of the autobiographical accounts written by adult sufferers have been eloquent and moving chronicles of life-long predicaments.* The dyslexic is apt to find himself an alien in a critical, if not hostile, *milieu*; mocked, misunderstood, or penalized; cut off from opportunities for advancement. Should the dyslexic child be of high intelligence, his prospects of developing neurotic reactions are all the greater, as he sees himself lagging behind junior members of his family, and younger companions. As an adolescent, the dyslexic occupies a ridiculous position especially in his contacts with the other sex, being handicapped socially, unable to read menus, programmes, film titles or news items; and incapable of receiving or writing letters. In adult life the dyslexic is bereft of intellectual and cultural advantages. Professional careers are barred. He is doomed to a second-class citizenship, for he is blind to the printed notices, instructions, appeals, exhortations, information and warnings which surround him. Rabinovitch *et al.* distinguishing primary from secondary types of reading retardation, believed that patients belonging to the latter group showed more symptoms of a "negative" character. Those with a primary reading retardation (who would correspond with our specific developmental dyslexics) reap the benefit of a high motivation to learn.

There is probably nothing specific or uniform about the neurotic pattern which may develop. The psychiatric features are often pleomorphic and unusual Nevertheless certain modes of reaction are commonly observed in boys who are dyslexic. Some of them display an excessive dependency upon their mothers, a reaction not unusual where the thwarted ambition of a father leads to a certain coldness towards the disappointing scholar. Another type of compensation is a channelling of attainment along some extra-curricular performance particularly games and athletics. Yet other dyslexics avoid losing face before their contemporaries by a process of clowning or waggery which allows them the licence of a classroom comedian. Perhaps the most unfortunate reaction and one which is by no means rare, is along the lines of aggression.

This last-named repercussion deserves particular notice. The ease

*See, for example, the letter written by Axel Rosendal (quoted by Hermann); the article by "X" in the *Brit. J. Ophth.*, 1936; Skydsgaard's account of the ex-word-blind lawyer; and the description retailed by Hermann, pp. 158–60.

with which a dyslexic teenager slips into delinquency demands serious notice. Von Holstein, a Danish High Court Judge, has made a special study of the correlation of word-blindness with criminal propensity. Pleading for a medico-legal recognition of the handicap of word-blindness he described the "martyrdom" and "frightful psychological trauma" endured by such children. Special classes for backward readers are regularly held in the Gatesville (Texas) State school for delinquent boys, where the incidence of dyslexia is high, especially among the coloured inmates, and those of Latin rather than "Anglo" racial stock.

Edmund Critchley (1968) who has particularly interested himself in the possibility of a correlation between dyslexia and juvenile delinquency, has investigated the incidence of reading-disability in a Remand Home and Classifying Centre for the twelve Inner London Boroughs. A series of 106 boys was studied prospectively, and 371 retrospectively, their ages ranging from 12 to 17 years (average 14 years 9 months). Approximately 60% of these delinquents were retarded in reading by two years or more, and 50% by over 3 years. Some of these were almost certainly cases of specific developmental dyslexia.

An Editorial in the periodical *Criminologist* (1968) dealt with the problem of dyslexia. The Editor made a rough survey by letters to probation and welfare officers in England and other European countries. One London probation officer replied "as a general impression most probation officers would certainly feel there was often a clear relationship between backwardness in reading and delinquent behaviour but I doubt if he would have any evidence as to how often the backwardness is caused by dyslexia." Another probation officer wrote '. . . one can certainly make the general comment that dyslexia is probably a contributory factor in quite a large number of cases". From Sweden a Welfare Officer wrote "my own work has shown a quite clear connection between this condition and juvenile delinquency, perhaps more than is suspected". The Editorial in *The Criminologist* concluded with the words "The broad feeling in the replies received by letter and verbally would indicate that the co-relation is familiar and that the prevalence of dyslexia as a cause or a contributing factor in juvenile delinquency may be considerable. There cannot be any doubt that a thorough survey and deep investigation by some responsible body is essential in this serious socio-educational problem".

Fortunately the neurotic reactions of dyslexics, however severe, are usually benign in character, for they readily yield to treatment once the underlying basis of difficulty in reading is realized and handled sympathetically.

The foregoing opinions as to the neurotic overlay are not universally held, however. Some still believe the neurotic picture to be clinically a specific one. The personality of the dyslexic has been described as immature, impulse-ridden and dependent, often misdiagnosed as postencephalitic, retarded or schizophrenic. The intelligence quotient may differ widely in the same child at different interviews. With the Rorschach test, dyslexics are said to be characterized by their pure colour responses; colour shock, poor form visualization; immaturity; disturbances in emotional development; and social adaptation (Gann, 1945).

According to Piaget, the age at which a normal child begins to read with facility is also the age at which he changes from an autistic, egocentric individual, to a societal, ethnocentric being. It has been suggested that successful learning in itself plays an important part in this normal phase of externalization (Wepman). The non-reader or dyslexic may continue for an undue length of time at his stage of autism. Perhaps this hypothesis goes some way towards explaining the occasional lapses into delinquency.

Some writers imply, even if they do not state explicitly, that the neurotic symptoms in poor readers are causal rather than reactionary. As might be expected, many psycho-analytic conjectures have in the past been put forward. To most who work among these children, assessing and assisting them in their difficulties, these notions smack of fantasy, and are of little value either in theory or in practice. One does not need to invoke the mythology of Oedipus who blinded himself, or of any notion of symbolic castration, to explain the difficulties experienced by the dyslexic child in sustaining attention upon his difficult, boring and unrewarding intellectual stint. That common-sense child psychiatrist Mildred Creak (1936) wrote "in so far as these children (i.e. poor readers) have any sort of emotional difficulty common to the group, it would seem to be an aversion to effort, showing itself in distractability, restlessness and lack of interest in books, and granted some common basis for the initial difficulty in reading, it is easy to see how the habitual evasion of that difficulty will set up faulty associations, and a persistence of these, until the mistakes become a habitual reaction".

The climate of opinion has considerably changed over the past five years, and those hypotheses which ascribed reading difficulties to psychogenic factors—at the same time denying the existence of dyslexia—are becoming out-moded. But for the unfortunate word-blind children and for their parents much remains to be done.

Even today some teachers and many child psychiatrists fail to realize that the neurotic symptoms which a dyslexic may show are secondary or reactionary. Only too often the backwardness in reading is deemed an environmental, psychogenic problem, causing a reluctance on the part of the child to persevere with the uphill task of learning his letters. So injustice is done. The specific defect is overlooked, and the dyslexic remains misunderstood and untaught.

Dyslexics who are of high intelligence and who are also lucky enough to retain their emotional stability, are sometimes capable of high achievement in later life. A dyslexic of sufficient ability, who is also fortunate in being endowed with unusual personality traits of application, concentration and ambition may in time overcome many of his problems even without specialized tuition. "Ego-strength" is what the psychiatrists call this quality, more familiar to us as "guts". If the specific disability has been recognized for what it is, the patient may lose many of his difficulties with reading, spelling and writing. Indeed it is a commonplace observation that once a dyslexic child is diagnosed as being the victim of a genuine inherent disability, and not a naughty, stupid, lazy or neurotic youngster, his self-respect is immediately enhanced, and any bad behaviour he may have shown, comes to an end, without intervention on the part of child psychiatry. Furthermore, under a regime of sympathetic and intensive coaching, resorting to an auditory system of learning, and fostering such potentialities as memory and quick associations, the dyslexic may still further advance in his schooling, and may even master or circumvent the screening processes which threaten to debar him from a career. According to one autobiographical account, an ex-dyslexic even attained high rank in the Foreign Office. One of Wernicke's patients became a lawyer. Another dyslexic is known to have become a surgeon who acquired his knowledge from lectures and bedside tuition rather than from books, and whose written work was legible enough to secure a pass. Yet another became an instructor in a Military Academy (Plate, 1909). Lloyd Thompson has suspected that such conspicuously successful men as Edison, Rodin, Harvey Cushing, George Patton, Woodrow Wilson, Lawrence Lowell, William James, and Albert Einstein, were "exdyslexics". As an offset, he also pointed to Harvey Lee Oswald in this connection. Even Nelson Rockefeller and the pioneer surgeon John Hunter have been suspected. The evidence here, it must be admitted, is equivocal.

On firmer grounds lies the belief that Hans Christian Andersen was also a dyslexic. He was very behind-hand in his school work, being regarded at one time as a dullard. Even as an adult he had never learned to spell correctly and his manuscripts revealed many errors of a type which are characteristic of dyslexia. Naturally enough these mistakes were usually detected and rectified by the editor. Occasionally, however, they escaped notice. Thus when Hans Christian Andersen wrote an account of his visit to Charles Dickens in London, names of English persons and places were often rendered incorrectly. These shortcomings were not always recognized by his publishers, so that they appeared in their original form in print. Among the numerous errors one may quote *Schackspeare*; *Machbeth*; *Tamps* or *Temps* (Thames); *Manschester*; *Brackfest* (breakfast).

Another retarded reader, possibly a dyslexic, was the Prince Imperial, son of Napoleon III. His tutors experienced great difficulty in teaching him to read and to write, though he was highly accomplished at sketching. He eventually passed into Woolwich and received a commission in the British army. In my possession there is the actual "reading machine" which was constructed for the Prince Imperial, and which was used by him at his lessons.

Chapter XIII
The nature of developmental dyslexia

We may attempt to sum up the opinions held currently by neurologists upon the topic of inherent reading difficulty in children. The problem is a considerable one and a complex one, for the total population of slow readers, retarded readers and poor readers, illiterates and semi-illiterates, is heterogenous. Monroe has spoken of a "constellation of factors in dyslexia", but perhaps it would be more accurate to refer to a constellation of subtypes. Any collected series will probably include some children who are dullards, if not indeed defectives. After all, if dyslexia is, as we believe, a constitutional and inborn problem, there is no reason why it should not affect all and sundry, irrespective of their intellectual rank or rating. Within this broad group of poor readers, a number of brain-injured may find themselves, the trauma dating from either pre- or post-natal life. Victims of neurological disease, not necessarily post-traumatic, may show conspicuous difficulty in learning to read. The overall population of retarded readers may also include some cases of disturbed or neurotic children whose emotional difficulties discourage learning. Educational progress may perhaps be handicapped by such unfavourable environmental circumstances as separation of parents, inconsistency of schooling, absenteeism through illness, delayed—or possibly even premature—attempts at teaching. The inherent nature of the language in question may play some part in bringing the reading defect to the notice of teachers at a very early age. Even such physical factors as minimal defects of hearing, refractive errors or ocular imbalance may hinder some children in their attempts to read, while inconsistent manual preference may impose still further hardship upon them when they try to write.

But all the foregoing are either epiphenomena or else irrelevancies. As we have already said, neurologists believe that within the community of poor readers there exists a hard core of cases where the origins of the learning defect are inborn and independent of any intellectual shortcomings which may happen to co-exist. Such are the cases which neurologists speak of as examples of specific, or developmental dyslexia. How large the problem is cannot be confidently stated until we are in possession of large-scale surveys of retarded readers, with a satisfactory analytic breakdown by neurologists and their team of ancillary experts.

To identify these cases of specific developmental dyslexia among the multitude of poor readers is no easy task. A wide experience is demanded of the diagnostician, together with a freedom from prejudice. Even so the isolation is still a difficult matter, for there is no single clinical feature which can be accepted as pathognomic. Diagnosis requires a battery of tests and a knowledge of the patient's family circumstances, his personality, and his environment. In other words, there must be an appraisal of a constellation of findings embracing positive as well as negative issues.

Many hypotheses have been mooted to "explain" specific dyslexia. The earlier observers were struck by the resemblance of their cases with the phenomena of aphasic alexia resulting from acquired disease. An agenesis of the cortex, involving especially the parietal lobes, was often invoked. As long ago as 1906, Claiborne envisaged an "imperfect development and tardy reaction of the word- and letter-memory cells" in the cerebral cortex, probably in the region of the left angular gyrus. Twenty years later, Bosworth McCready regarded dyslexic cases as being due to ontogenetic causes—a biological variation or stigma of degeneration, similar to colour-blindness and defective ocular fusion sense. Later the author modified his views, believing that birth-trauma might be all-important.

Many such speculations are of mere historical interest.

Orton's theory of visual rivalry from inadequate unilateral occipital suppression is on the face of it too speculative. This idea does not explain why dimensions should be confused in a lateral direction only. Nor does it give any reason why verbal symbol-arrangement alone is at fault, while surrounding objects, scenes and pictures appear in normal orientation.

Any theory of minimal brain damage, whether or not sustained *in utero*, is also unconvincing. In the first place it conflicts with the factor of inheritance. It does not explain those cases where neurological deficits cannot be demonstrated even after the most searching techniques. Furthermore the plasticity of the nervous system in the young might be expected to compensate for the effects of any circumscribed lesion of very early appearance. No brain-pathology has indeed ever been demonstrated in a case of developmental dyslexia, though this is an argument of lesser weight, for there is a striking absence of any autopsy material whatsoever.

Some writers have looked upon developmental dyslexia as not altogether a "specific" entity, but merely one aspect of inadequate achievement of the faculty of language. Thus a form of congenital "aphasia" has been envisaged, comparable with the disabilities which may follow acquired disease of the brain. As we have seen, these analogies have been stressed from the earliest days and are illustrated in the original term "congenital word-blindness". Just as modern aphasiologists look askance at any conception of pure or isolated alexia in adult cases, so too some writers insist that closer investigation of developmental dyslexics will always uncover other defects of a linguistic order. In particular, motor impairments of speech have been stressed. Whether these be simply articulatory in character, or whether they lie at a higher level within the realm of language, or both, is not always made clear. Thus Monroe, who was impressed by the frequency of deviant speech in poor readers, thought that the two were causally related. Inaccurate diction, she said, might cause a confused association of sounds with printed symbols. A child who has an articulatory defect hears the word as spoken by others in one way, and as spoken by himself, in another. Eisenson (1958) also stressed the possible detriment of faulty diction to learning, in that errors of pronunciation may cause difficulties in recognizing printed words. The child's own concern over his manner of talking may hinder him from concentrating upon the meaning of what he reads aloud, and so lead to inadequate understanding. Furthermore, a speech disorder like stuttering which disturbs the rate and rhythm of speaking, may also impair phrasing, and interfere with the comprehension of written symbols.

Some of these contributions betray an obvious confusion between imperfections of articulation or speech, and higher order deficiencies within the realm of language.

But there are weighty objections to the concept of developmental dyslexia as a fragment of congenital "aphasia". The idea is a specious one which must be scrutinized with caution. In the first place we know very little about the nature of the so-called congenital "aphasias". It would be better to speak in terms of a mere comparison with cases of loss of language in the adult or older child, and not to try and exalt an analogy to the status of a hypothesis. The comparison has a certain utilitarian merit, but no more. Profound psychological, linguistic and philosophical differences exist between the problem of a developmental dyslexic, and that of an adult who has long ago acquired language in the usual way, and then lost it. The latter has been using it as a communicative tool for so many years that he has developed his own individual associations and has unwittingly built up a veritable idiolect. His vocabulary, available as well as utilized, is rich, extensive and replete with memory-traces and over-tones. The linguistic armamentarium may even include patterns from other cultures, as well as certain non-verbal systems of communication. Language has thus grown to be an integral built-in part of an adult's personality, and his use of language has become a highly specific aspect of his total behaviour. In such a person, circumscribed brain-disease may impair this complex patterning, but the effect will bear only a superficial resemblance to the child who is slow in achieving this same faculty. Actually there is a vast difference between the problem of a mature and possibly scholarly adult who, as the result of a brain-lesion, finds it difficult by sweeping his gaze quickly over a line of print to utilize critical details and contextual associations so as to identify the meaning of the text in the rough. At times even individual morphemes, words or phrases cannot be interpreted. The acquired dyslexic shares with the developmental dyslexic a certain lack of facility in the full appreciation of verbal symbols; but there the likeness rests, and the analogy should not be pressed further.

Moreover, an acquired alexic may sometimes retain his ability to write. More often, however, he finds it hard to express his ideas on paper, and to draw upon what was previously a very rich vocabulary, without betraying hesitancies, repetitions, omissions and corrections. The graphic efforts of a child with developmental dyslexia are fundamentally different, and resemblances between the two kinds of dysgraphia will not stand up to scrutiny. To speak of a "congenital dysgraphia" in the context of a developmental dyslexia, is not appropriate.

It is still necessary to emphasize these points despite the fact that they were clearly stated as long ago as 1903 at the *Société de Neurologie de Paris*, when Foerster presented the case of an imbecile who could not read. In the discussion which ensued, the topic of illiteracy among children was raised. Mme. Dejerine stressed that it was important not to confuse the pathological loss of a function with cases of absence of that function. Pierre Marie agreed, and went on to assert, "*je ne crois pas que les troubles de la lecture observés chez nos malades soient en-rien comparables à ceux de l'aphasie vraie*".

The contemporary theory of cerebral immaturity, or maturational lag, is the hypothesis which demands the most serious attention. According to Werner and Kaplan (1963) maturation comprises a process of growth from unstable and primitive to stable and highly integrated hierarchic behaviour. A developmental dyslexic is often regarded in American parlance as a "late bloomer", but only in regard to the flowering of certain specific faculties. The frequent occurrence of cortical equipotentiality, or rather, the lack of distinct unilateral cerebral dominance, is adduced as supporting evidence. Electroencephalographic data may also be quoted as being consonant with a state of cortical immaturity. Bender was one of the first to propound this theory, which she pleaded with eloquence. She regarded the notion as being based on a concept of functional areas of the brain and of personality developing according to a recognized pattern. A maturational lag signifies a slow differentiation within this pattern. It does not imply any structural defect, deficiency, or loss. Potentialities are not necessarily limited, and, at various levels, maturation may speed up, though unevenly so. These cases are understandable in terms of "embryonic plasticity"; i.e. as yet unformed, but capable of being formed; being impressionable and responsive to patterning, with the implication of designs as yet unfixed.

This attractive hypothesis raises certain questions. If specific developmental dyslexia represents a peculiar type of cerebral immaturity, it follows that the difficulty in reading might eventually improve—provided, of course, that attempts to learn are continued long enough. But of course the opportunities for learning slip by all too quickly. More information is needed here. Developmental dyslexia is certainly not often diagnosed in adulthood even though genuine instances are encountered from time to time. One naturally asks why they should be so uncommon. Perhaps the patient and his parents have resigned themselves to a state of hopeless ineducability, and no longer importune doctors and teachers. The victims may have merged into the amorphous population of adult illiterates and semi-illiterates. Maybe he has eventually made such improvement as to achieve modest social and economic adjustment, but remains a poor speller, an unwilling correspondent, and a reluctant reader. Finally, it is conceivable that the childhood dyslexic—the slow bloomer—eventually matures and blossoms, so as no longer to be conspicuously handicapped.

Obviously large-scale longitudinal or follow-up studies are needed of those in whom the diagnosis of developmental dyslexia has been made in childhood by experienced neurologists.

The second problem which emerges from this hypothesis of maturational lag concerns the nature of the precise faculties involved. It is hard to avoid the conclusion that mere visual non-identification of verbal symbols is not the whole story. Not only is it a matter of defective perception, but it is also one of inadequate high-level co-ordination of lexical percepts. Clearly there is also a tie-up between the recognition of the form of a visual symbol and its acoustic properties. This process of linking one percept with another is where the principal fault may lie. As Vernon has emphasized, there is in reading-retardation a failure in analysis, abstraction and generalization, within the linguistic sphere. The cerebral activity which lags behind in maturation may be a specific cognitive act in which verbal symbols, acoustic as well as visual, fail to achieve identity.

The auditory component in the pathogenesis of dyslexia was foreshadowed by Fildes and by Bronner. Marshall and Ferguson (1939) spoke of a difficulty in remembering the mental picture of a word, though general memory is excellent . . . "(The dyslexic) just can't see meanings unless he can hear the word". The same writers spoke of dyslexia in terms of a sensori-motor integrative disability at the highest, or "skill" level. The word-blind are limited chiefly by their inability to circumvent the faulty visual associations of speech by acoustic as well as other channels.

Money (1962) surmised that the dyslexic, in his difficulty in establishing lexical concepts, visual and auditory, may be of a non-visile cognitional type, possibly weak in visual representation and visual memory, the opposite of one endowed with a photographic eidetic imagery.

Earlier still, and in a more elaborate fashion, Schilder expressed some of these same ideas. He traced the basic difficulty to an inability to differentiate the spoken word into its component sounds, and to put the sounds together so as to constitute a word. Spoken words and phonemes when brought into connection with a written word and a written letter cannot be integrated and differentiated. This failure may be witnessed when a dyslexic, shown the word "banana" for instance, fails to grasp its meaning. Directed to spell the word aloud, letter by letter, the dyslexic may correctly proclaim "B.A.N.A.N.A." but still be quite unable either to understand it or to pronounce it. Schilder also referred to the common occurrence of mirror-opposite mistakes and other errors in the optic perception of letters. Dyslexia, he said, was an isolated disorder within a gnostic-intellectual function.

The role of maturational lag in developmental dyslexia has been further elaborated by Birch (1962). Regarding perceptual levels, Birch concluded that a normal child passes through the consecutive stages of discrimination, analysis, and synthesis. This perceptual evolution is sensitive to brain-damage. One of the problems which contribute to a reading disability is an inadequate achievement of the higher and complex levels of visuo-perceptual function. Birch predicted that among those with a reading-disability one should be able to identify certain patients with defective analytic and synthetic visuo-perceptual capacity. A complementary hypothesis discussed by Birch visualized a hierarchy among the sensory systems. For reading readiness it is essential that the visual system should become dominant. Children who possess a different type of sensory protocol, make up a type with reading disability. The evolution of behaviour can be "conceptualized" as the process of development of intersensory patterning. Some victims of reading-disability have impaired equivalences between the sensory systems. Birch believed that most children with reading problems find it difficult to establish visuo-auditory-equivalences, and perhaps also visuo-kinaesthetic and visuo-tactuo-kinaesthetic relations. His experimental findings supported this belief, and he considered that his way of looking upon the problem of dyslexia might uncover important mechanisms.

To a clinical neurologist certain dysfunctions are recalled which are commonly regarded as being parieto-occipital in character. The not infrequent conjunction of dyslexia with directional disorders and with spatial defects, both of a personal and an extra-personal nature, may be cited as suggestive evidence. In so far as symbolic thinking is at fault in these dyslexic patients, it is the parieto-occipital region of the dominant hemisphere which is under suspicion, that is if one can discern any firm cerebral dominance at all.

There are some who, looking behind the maturational inadequacy seek to invoke a more fundamental defect in Gestalt recognition.

Visuo-verbal comprehension is naturally impaired. The spatial disorders, reversals in reading and in writing, mixed hand-eye preferences,
and other problems which may be met with in dyslexics are, according
to Drew (1956), "variant manifestations in the fundamental defect in
correct figure-ground recognition". Drew believed that "the incon-
sistencies, confusion, and apparently diametrically opposed findings
reported in the literature and observed clinically can best be resolved
by interpreting the findings in a configurational setting".

A marble-board test for figure-background discrimination has been
devised by Klapper. However a fairly extensive trial among my cases
has not shown it to be a useful tool in the clinical detection of dyslexia.

The adoption of some such theory of late blooming in a specific
sense leads on to the question whether other specialized instances of
maturational lag are ever encountered in neuro-paediatric practice. A
possible analogy with congenital auditory imperception, constitutional
dyscalculia, and also with congenital apraxia immediately comes to
mind. Constitutional colour-blindness, and lack of musical ear, are
more questionable analogues, for these shortcomings are permanent
rather than transient, and a maturational lag seems a scarcely tenable
explanation here.

Does a specific cerebral immaturity imply a structural lesion,
recognizable by present-day techniques? Probably not, though the
question still cannot be answered with complete confidence. Certain
contributors would seem to infer that some form of brain-pathology,
traumatic or otherwise, lies at the foundation of the pathogenesis of
dyslexia, whether it be regarded as a dyssymbolia, or a maturational
lag. The lack of autopsy data is a regrettable *lacuna* in our knowledge
of developmental dyslexia. Even though it seems unlikely that any
tangible evidence will emerge, it is clearly desirable for the record that
pathological studies should be made and published on children who
have been earlier diagnosed as instances of developmental dyslexia.
We recall that in the case of congenital auditory imperception, post-
mortem study proved to be entirely negative as regards cerebral
pathology.

The notion of a cerebral immaturity also raises the rather remote
possibility of an underlying genetically determined bio-chemical
dyscrasia. The analogy of constitutional histidinaemia comes to mind, in
that this particular inborn error of amino-acid metabolism is associated
with a conspicuous retardation in speech-development. Obviously it
would be unwise to neglect chemical aspects in any research into the
aetiology of dyslexia.

Do clinical sub-types exist within the narrow neurological category
of specific developmental dyslexia? This idea is currently popular,
though the supporting evidence is not yet convincing. For example it
is sometimes considered that one dyslexic may show a conspicuous

problem in the visual sphere, while another may present with greater difficulties of an acoustic order. Yet a third dyslexic may be beset with both types of problem in approximately equal measure.

Proceeding from such conceptions, there has arisen an attempt to devise certain profiles whereby clusters of disabilities are associated, each forming an alleged sub-syndrome of developmental dyslexia. Thus the auditory sub-type is said to include cases where the acquisition of speech was late; where the acoustic discrimination and memory of phonemes and words are faulty; where the naming of objects is imperfect; and where the verbal I.Q. falls below the level of the performance I.Q. in the W.I.S.C. test. By way of contrast there is alleged to exist a dyslexic sub-syndrome where visual perception and memory are weak; where there is difficulty in differentiating complicated visual figures; where the subject fails the Bender visual Gestalt test; and where the performance I.Q. is lower than the verbal I.Q. on W.I.S.C. testing. Other minor neuro-psychological deficits are often associated with the one sub-type or the other.

Clearly these are interesting ideas but today they cannot be regarded as more than expressions of opinion.

The question as to whether clear cut sub-types genuinely exist is of some pragmatic importance when it comes to remedial teaching. Would it be appropriate to tailor the technique to the child? Or should each dyslexic be squeezed into the Procrustean bed of one uniform remedial panacea, whether the technique be that proposed by Norrie, Gillingham, Frostig, Chassagny, Borel-Maisonny, for example?

It is, indeed, in the classroom rather than the Clinic, where the tendency occurs to speak in terms of sub-types.

Just how these sub-types are isolated and how precise are the little syndromes within dyslexia, is still perhaps a project for further inquiry rather than immediate acceptance.

Before adopting wholeheartedly the conception of sub-types, it is necessary to recall that a spurious appearance of diversity may result merely from the interplay of a veritable constellation of factors, some of them endogenous, others exogenous. For example, the parental attitude towards their child's dyslexia may vary from one family to another. Some parents quickly come to realize that a very real and puzzling disability exists, and they go to great pains to deal with the problem, tackling teachers who may be critical or merely bored. Other parents react by overt disappointment, lack of sympathy, or intolerance. The attitude of school-teachers to the late reader is also inconsistent, and some are frankly cruel in their handling of dyslexics. Too frequent chopping and changing of schools is another detrimental factor which is at times unavoidable. This is mirrored in the apparently high incidence of dyslexia in the offspring of diplomats, active Service personnel and missionaries. The child's own response to his difficulty in learning

D.C.

to read differs from case to case, and this may influence the clinical picture. A dyslexic of above average I.Q., who is also endowed with unusual personality traits of ambition, doggedness and application may in time overcome much of his disability in a measure which is beyond one with lesser potentials in the way of intellect and Ego-strength.

Other variables which enter the scene, and which may alter the dyslexia to the extent of suggesting diversity rather than uniformity, are the age at which the diagnosis is established; the socio-cultural status of the family; the factor of plurilingualism; the nature of the earliest teaching-technique; and the innate linguistic properties of the language concerned.

Chapter XIV
The dyslexic child grows up

That dyslexics are totally incapable of learning to read is a fallacy which seems to have been at one time widely accepted among educationalists. Neurologists do not agree with this *non possumus* viewpoint and have explicitly and repeatedly said so ever since the days of Hinshelwood (1917). Admittedly the prognosis may be more serious in developmental dyslexics than in cases of psychogenic reading-retardation, but the outlook is anything but hopeless. With appropriate tuition dyslexics can make considerable progress and they may attain sufficient ability to read for all practical purposes. Even without such skilled assistance, they may often spontaneously improve. That is to say they become able to interpret notices, advertisements, newsprint and letters, even though they will probably remain recalcitrant slow readers. Many ex-dyslexics, left to their own devices, perhaps never became "bookish", and may but rarely peruse a novel or magazine as a form of recreation, and for the sheer fun of it.

However, in the absence of organized skilled instruction, dyslexics are usually left to fend for themselves. Many of the less fortunate among them drift in an educational sense, and simply become items within the community of illiterates or near-illiterates. As such they will be barred from any lucrative or worthwhile profession and they will have to be content with work of a manual or practical kind. The victim may be rated fortunate if he does not swell the ranks of the delinquent or the anti-social.

The two following case-reports illustrate the type of *niche* into which a stable and not unintelligent dyslexic will fit, in the absence of specific tuition.

P.M., male, aged 31 years, was never able to learn to read though good at most other subjects, and indeed top of the school in handicrafts. He left school at the age of 14 and served with the R.A.F. for 2 years. There he constantly confused right and left on the parade ground: he was unable to learn the Morse code for signalling purposes. One of the officers used to write his letters for him. He made close friends with another airman who was also dyslexic. On his return to civilian life he took a job as a dental mechanic which he held for 7 years. During that time he was able to memorize and recall the dental formulae of all his employer's patients. He could drive a car well and comprehend the wayside road-signs and traffic-signals. Although unable to read a map properly, or to understand the sign-posts, he was able to motor all over England without getting lost. Similarly he could usually identify the individual discs in his collection of gramophone records. On Raven's progressive matrices he scored 32 out of 60; his I.Q. was estimated to be 93. No neurological abnormality could be demonstrated but his ocular movements during the act of attempting to read were found by appropriate test-methods to be very abnormal (see Fig. 36). An E.E.G. revealed no pathological rhythms.

L.G., a coloured female aged 21 years was the youngest of five children. She attended a primary school in Trinidad but could never master the art of reading and was bottom in her class in this subject and also in spelling and writing to dictation. At arithmetic, history and English she was rated as average. This inability to read was a source of great distress to her, and on leaving school at the age of 16 years she went to work with the express intention of saving enough money to go to England to learn to read. After 4 years she had accumulated sufficient for her fare. On her own initiative and without the help of friends or relatives in the Caribbean or in England she took passage in a ship and came to live and work in London, where she knew no one. She secured a job in a factory as a rag-sorter and then sought help from her doctor as to her reading-disability. Although unable to read she could find her way around London by comparing the number or destination of a bus with a pencilled note which a neighbour had given her. When shopping she would match the graphic symbols on the packages with those on her shopping list. Confronted with a printed word she might at times identify and read aloud correctly the constituent letters without, however, being able to name or to recognize the meaning of the word as a whole.

In other respects the patient was perfectly normal and no neurological deficit could be detected. Her writing to dictation is shown in Fig. 20. The formal intelligence quotient was given as 65, but this was certainly a serious underestimate due to lack of socio-cultural *rapport* with the psychometrist.

Arrangements were made for this patient to be employed in the hospital as a ward-maid (where she proved highly efficient) and for her to receive tuition in reading at the hands of the Chaplain (no facilities being available within the sphere of the Ministry of Education).

In exceptionally auspicious circumstances, a dyslexic may fare better as he grows older, even though unassisted. This fact has been touched upon in the previous chapter. Given a good intellectual level, constancy of purpose, emotional stability and drive, the dyslexic may in later life manage to achieve such a modicum of literacy as to enable him to occupy a modest *niche* within the wage-earning community. He may even be lucky enough to benefit from some coaching at the hands of a sympathetic even if untrained teacher. Provided that the tuition is individual and intensive a partial success may reward unskilled or semi-skilled instruction at the hands of someone like a retired school-teacher or parson.

In the next three cases, family circumstances were probably instrumental in securing for the dyslexic a relatively good adjustment in adulthood.

J.P., male, aged 33 years, had always experienced difficulty in learning to read. His two daughters were also retarded readers. In other respects his scholastic achievements were of at least average level. He attended a public school of an unorthodox sort, and then went to an Agricultural College. He managed to pass the first two examinations out of a possible three, and in his studies he relied entirely upon lectures and demonstrations—text-books being impracticable. The patient now runs his own farm with complete success. Reading is managed with extreme slowness but he can cope with the ordinary circulars and news-headings. On reading aloud he was found to fare better with the longer nouns, verbs and adjectives, while frequently stumbling over the short mono-syllabic words, such as the articles, conjunctions and prepositions. His handwriting was neat but barely legible, and many odd errors in spelling were to be seen.

M.M., female, aged 21 years, had attended an ordinary infant school, and from the start she experienced difficulty in learning to read. At first she was deemed to be lazy. Later she was suspected as being in need of glasses and these were ordered. In turn she went to a primary school, a private school and a secondary modern school, leaving at the age of 16 years. It was only when she went to a convent school in Singapore that something unusual was realized to be the matter with her. At no time did she see anyone from the Ministry of Education, although she was examined in a routine fashion by school medical officers, who "did not seem very interested". She sat her 11-plus examination, but failed because she could not read the test-papers. When she left school she worked at a nursery *crêche*, and then trained as a nurse for 2 years. She had to give this up, for the sister-tutor could never read her lecture-notes. She then spent a year among handicapped children, and now she is a nursing auxilliary at a mental hospital.

The difficulty in reading has persisted although she has mastered her defect up to a point: that is to say she can now read to the extent of beginning to look at books for her own pleasure though it takes her a very long time to study a page. She prefers magazines and short stories. From the start she found script more difficult than print and she could not consistently identify the ownership or various specimens of writing. She could always recognize numerals, but she was never adept at arithmetic. She can read traffic signs in the street, and she can follow T.V. and the cinema— except foreign films where she cannot fathom the English sub-titles because they are exposed for too short a period of time. Rarely does she venture upon cross-word puzzles.

Even today the patient's handwriting is very untidy and barely legible, with frequent spelling mistakes of an unusual character (see Figs. 16, 17, 18). Certain characters are at times written in an unorthodox fashion. Sometimes two adjacent letters are not joined together; on other occasions they may be connected in an odd manner. Capital letters are sometimes incongruously interpolated and dots may be replaced by dashes. Occasionally she reverses a short word, as for example "if" which she writes as "fi". Finally strange mistakes in spelling are often made involving not only long words, but also short words which should be familiar.

The patient declared herself to be right-handed, but she wore her wrist-watch on the right arm like many sinistrals, and she folded her arms in a typical left-handed fashion. She stated that at one time she used to muddle up hopelessly her right and her left.

A.C., female, aged 18 years, a member of a dyslexic family, had herself been severely retarded in learning to read. By dint of great application coupled with a background of high intelligence, she had largely mastered her disability though she never learned to spell correctly. A brilliant violinist, she was considerably handi-capped at the Royal College because of her persistent inability to read musical notation.

Within such a category of well adjusted ex-dyslexics may belong the case of Karl XI (1655–97) who has been judged "one of Sweden's wisest kings". Succeeding to the throne at the age of 4 years he proved to be a most unsatisfactory scholar, mainly because of his inability to learn to read. His studies were supervized by a Professor of History at the University of Uppsala. The monarch's progress in reading was extraordinarily slow, and in adult life he always relied upon personal interviews rather than a study of reports. If handed a document he might be seen to hold the page upside-down and to pretend that he was reading the text. Throughout his life his spelling was highly unorthodox, the errors being quite unlike the usual mis-spellings of the uneducated. He would reverse words, omit letters, or start with letters belonging to the middle of a word. Perusal of his journals and *aides-mémoire* brings to light a number of startling mistakes: e.g. "ta" for *att*; "faton" for *aftou;* "wathen"', for *staden;* "aagt" for *gott;* "arrgdh" for *gård;* "kråken" for *klockan;* "nathet" for *natten;* "tu" for *tva;* "byggnadshjalp" for *bygginshielp,* and "recyteran" for *rekryter.* Reversals and other such spelling mistakes were habitual with him up to the time of his death.

Obviously it is most unsatisfactory that dyslexics should remain neglected as well as unrecognized; or that they should be allowed merely to muddle through as best they can. The disability is one which is amenable to treatment provided this be carried out with sufficient intensity, patience, sympathy and understanding. Perhaps, indeed, these qualities are more necessary to the teacher than any special pedagogic trick of technique or skill. The system of teaching which is adopted may matter less than the manner in which the instruction is imparted.

Sharp expressed this well when he wrote . . . "More important . . . than the training itself . . . is the quality of the teacher. Given the basic background and knowledge required to the handling of remedial cases, there is no substitute in the teacher for personality, a degree of missionary spirit, versatility, the pedagogical flair, patience, understanding, and the courage of one's convictions. When we consider the nature of the language disability and the complexity of language learning, it seems to me obvious that there is no one remedial method yet evolved which can be offered to teachers on a silver platter" (1951).

Nevertheless it is hard to escape the conclusion that it is important to the dyslexic (and to the community) for his disability to be recognized for what it is: and for unpropitious ways and circumstances of teaching to be avoided in favour of more appropriate methods. The dyslexic child obviously should no longer be taught in a large class where he is apt to find himself a cynosure and a butt. His reading lessons must be held in private, and his reading material should be interesting, even stimulating in nature.

Should this educational regime be carried out at special schools, or in ordinary schools by way of a specialist teacher? Thus, on the one hand it might be deemed best to establish a number of educational establishments, either residential or non-residential, which would cater exclusively for dyslexic children. The example of schools for the deaf, the blind, and the speech-retarded comes to mind immediately. Our ignorance of the exact size of the dyslexic problem makes it hard to gauge whether or not this plan would be unnecessarily extravagant.

The alternative would be to establish a corps of selected teachers who have been trained in the specific educational techniques appropriate for the dyslexic. These could then serve as peripatetic specialist teachers who would cover the schools within a region, and who would cope with selected pupils in a quiet and encouraging environment. This second method seems to be the more desirable. Obviously as a necessary preliminary to such an organization, a systematic diagnostic or screening service would be necessary, whereby dyslexic children could be identified within the population of dullards, neurotics, and slow readers.

The Danish system of training dyslexics which was instituted in 1935–36, may be quoted, although obviously the problem may not be the same in all countries. In Hellerup, one of the suburbs of Copenhagen, a large private house was converted into a non-residential *Ordblinde Institut*. The school copes with 100 pupils, the children entering at the age of 9 or 10 years. The duration of training averages two years. The pupils live at home and travel to and from the school in State supplied transport. In the case of children who live outside Copenhagen, lodgings are found near the institution. Tuition continues for 5 hours a day, 6 days a week. The daily curriculum comprises reading and writing (2 hours); arithmetic (1 hour); singing, drawing or handicraft (1 hour); and some other subject (1 hour). The classes for reading and writing are made up of 3 pupils to a teacher: in the case of arithmetic, however, the class may include as many as 12.

The teachers at the Institute previously have undergone special post-graduate training (lasting 2 to 3 months) for which they receive an additional diploma.

Early cases of dyslexia are selected at the ordinary schools where the classes ordinarily comprise 30 to 35 children. Those children who prove to be slow at learning to read are first of all referred to a special "reading class" within the ordinary school, where the pupils number 16 to one teacher. If, while in this class, the child is suspected of being a true dyslexic, he is referred to a diagnostic centre in Copenhagen. There a decision is made whether the scholar should be sent to the Word-Blind Institute.

Most word-blind children come under the auspices of the State and pay no fees. However, if the parents so wish, the pupils can also attend the Institute in a private capacity, the fees being 135 Kr. a month (£7 10s. 0d.).

After ordinary school hours, extension classes are held on the Institute premises until 9 p.m., for the benefit of adolescents and adults whose prior education in reading has been neglected. Two hundred such adults usually attend. As a rule the tuition is free but pupils can also be accepted on a private basis, the fees being 25 Kr. (£1 7s. 0d.) a month, comprising 2 hours a week.

In addition to the *Ordblinde Institut* there is a continuation school (*Hellerup-hus Efterskole*) close by. This caters on a non-residential basis for those of 14 years of age or more who need further help with reading and writing. This course of instruction lasts one year and the curriculum comprises 6 hours a day. Ordinarily the State is responsible for the fees but here again private pupils may be accepted who pay 80 Kr. (£4 8s. 0d.) a month, for 6 to 8 hours a day.

The staff comprises 40 teachers, 20 being full-time and 20 part-time, and the teachers are shared between the two institutes. In addition there exists in Denmark an official register of these specially trained teachers of the word-blind who will accept private patients.

Various specialized ways of teaching dyslexics have from time to time been advanced, e.g. the Norrie phonetic system, the Orton-Gillingham-Stillman technique, and the Borel-Maisonny gestural method. There are others, of course. Perhaps there is no single specific method of tuition. Orton himself was of the opinion that "anything that will work is a good method". Maybe the teaching requires to be modified to suit the individual dyslexic. This ties up with the question of possible sub-types, as already discussed. If it is true that even within the nucleus of cases of developmental dyslexia situated at the core of the diverse pupils with reading problems, clinical sub-types exist, then it may well be that no one technique suffices.

The exact methods of teaching constitute a technical side of pedagogy which cannot be discussed in a work such as this. Certain general principles can, however, be stressed.

(1) The "look and say" method of reading should be replaced by a more phonic or analytic-synthetic system in the case of dyslexics.

(2) The progression from simple tasks to more complex ones should be made slowly and gradually.

(3) Visual learning should be reinforced by other sense-channels. Thus the dyslexic child should be taught to learn the appearances of a letter (or word); to say the symbol aloud; to trace its outlines digitally; and to write it down.

(4) The reading-material chosen for learning purposes should be interesting and exciting for the young reader, so as to increase the motivation to continue with the task.

(5) Toys, incorporating letters and words, should be encouraged as a sort of ancillary play-therapy.

(6) The teaching should be individual and intense, but each session should be relatively short, i.e. not longer than 30 minutes.

(7) Mechanical aids may be employed to help the reader keep his place in a printed text, e.g. a marker, or even a finger-tip.

There is also a place among the techniques for instruction, for certain mechanical aids. Various "reading machines" have been devised, culminating in the elaborate "talking typewriter". Tape-recorders and gramophone records are often serviceable in the case of the older dyslexics, especially of the type whereby English is taught to foreigners. Even a simple typewriter is of service in that it assists the poor speller in achieving a clear visual image of the correct appearance of a word.

In order that the child may concentrate upon learning to read, write and spell, some subject or subjects may require to be sacrificed from the school curriculum. Thus it may well be considered more important for the dyslexic to concentrate upon the basic subjects so difficult to him, than to try and cope with some less essential subject such as Latin, French, or algebra. Purely oral instruction in a foreign language is not objectionable, but unfortunately a proficiency in spoken French does not usually satisfy the examiners in the Common Entrance Examination.

In uncomplicated cases of dyslexia, i.e. where no serious neurotic problem exists, psychological treatment is unnecessary or even perhaps unwise. The practice which was recently in vogue of referring dyslexics to a Child Guidance Clinic, is not good enough. It is skilled tuition which is required, not psychotherapy. In this connection Joss, Leiman and Schiffman (1961) quoted an experimental series of 40 children with reading problems. They were divided into 4 groups of ten. One group received remedial reading and psychotherapy only; and the fourth group received no treatment at all. The results seemed—as far as they were reliable—to favour the role of remedial reading.

Although crossed laterality is not uncommon in dyslexics, it is not necessary nor indeed advisable to attempt to change the retarded reader's handedness, eyedness, or footedness. Motor exercises devised to improve the child's co-ordination or physical efficiency play no serious role in the re-education of the dyslexic.

These last two sentences are expressed in order to counter the techniques for training poor readers which for a time had a certain vogue in parts of the United States. For a critical appraisal of the Delacato treatment of dyslexics the reader is referred to an important review in Neurology 1964. 14. 559; to the monograph written by O'Donnell (1969); and in particular to the official *pronunciamento* in Neurology 1968. 18. 1214.

Some have advocated that remedial instruction of dyslexics should be preceded by a 6-month regime of visual, auditory, and tactile training. The reason for this is not clear, and it would seem to affront commonsense not to institute specialized courses of reading as soon as possible.

These remarks upon remediation lead naturally to considerations as to prognosis. What does the future hold for dyslexics? Naturally enough this depends upon very many factors: the intellectual level; the date of recognition; Ego-strength; the attitude of parents, siblings, and school-teachers; and the availability of skilled tuition. It has already been stated, and because of frequent mis-quotation, it needs to be asserted again, that *a dyslexic child can be taught to read*.

To look still further ahead: what academic success are the dyslexics capable of achieving? We have already referred to the examples of well-known persons who have attained distinction in various fields, despite an initial problem with reading. But it may be objected that such individuals were non-specific retarded readers rather than dyslexics. It may also be suggested that these were exceptional cases. The increasing handicap of academic hurdles in the way of "O" and "A" levels and other types of artificial assessments, may constitute a barrier which dyslexics of yesterday never had to contend with. It would be of greater value to take a population of known dyslexics, and to follow up their subsequent careers.

At the simplest end of the scale one may quote Monroe's figures for the results of treatment of children with retarded reading. It must be recalled that Monroe did not accept the concept of dyslexia though her series must surely have included a number of such cases. Eighty-nine children who were poor readers received remedial training under close supervision: of these 93% made "accelerated progress" and 5% made normal progress. Of 50 children who received remedial instruction in reading, but at their own schools from their own teachers, 52% made accelerated progress and 14% made a normal progress. Of another 50 children who received no remedial instruction in reading at all, none made accelerated progress; 4% made normal progress; and 96% made "retarded progress'.

Although dating from 10 years ago, the figures obtained from a follow-up study at the Copenhagen Word-Blind Institute merit quotation (see Table IV).

Follow-up studies have since been made by Robinson and Smith (1962), Silver and Hagin (1964), Barlow and Blomquist (1965), and Preston and Yarrington (1966). Obviously far more work is needed along these lines. The difficulties are not inconsiderable, for an extended longitudinal study of dyslexics who were originally diagnosed on firm grounds sufficiently long ago, must be hard to achieve.

A particularly hopeful note is struck on reading Rawson's follow-up account (1968) of 20 dyslexic boys. All these had attended the same private school, and because of their difficulties with reading had received remedial teaching according to the Orton-Gillingham-Stillman system. Two of these boys did eventually become college graduates. Four achieved bachelor's degrees; four had each added one year of graduate study; one attained a law degree; one a graduate degree in divinity. Three others—already with Master's degrees—were doctoral candidates. Five had already been granted doctor's degrees, one of these had put in a two year post-doctoral study. Another had gained a Ph.D. in addition to his M.D. The occupations held by these 20 ex-dyslexics were as follows: Doctor (medical) 2 (both research scientists and one also a Ph.D. in bio-chemistry and a college professor); lawyer 1; college professor 2 (one a departmental head); research scientist (non-medical) 2; owner medium business 3; "middle management" 3; school principal 1; secondary school teacher 3 (one with M.A., two with B.A.); actor (in regular employment under contract) 1; factory foreman 1; skilled labourer, in training, 1. Had the author

TABLE IV
PUPILS AND GRADUATES OF THE
COPENHAGEN WORD-BLIND INSTITUTE
(1935–36)

Total	Present Status	Born 1924 or earlier	Born 1925 –1929	Born 1930 –1934	Born 1935 or later
84	Still attending school.	1	2	41	40
23	⎡ Passed entrance examination, Institute of Higher Education	—	1	2	2
	⎢ Students, I.H. Ed.	1	10	2	—
	⎣ Graduates, I.H. Ed.	1	4	—	—
16	⎡ Passed entrance examination, Teachers' College	—	—	1	2
	⎣ Students, Teachers' College	1	2	8	2
8	Kindergarten teachers	1	1	3	3
5	Other types of teacher-training	1	3	1	—
29	⎡ Student nurses .	2	6	11	1
	⎢ Nurses .	3	1	—	—
	⎣ Children's nurses	—	2	3	—
48	⎡ Shop assistants.	1	2	3	—
	⎢ Trainees .	2	3	18	14
	⎣ Higher executives	2	1	1	1
25	Clerical work ⎡ Junior clerks.	—	1	6	3
	⎣ Clerks .	4	2	7	2
86	Skilled workers ⎡ Apprentices .	—	5	22	17
	⎣ Artisans .	16	12	13	1
69	Unskilled workers ⎡ Labourers .	9	8	3	2
	⎢ Factory workers, storemen .	4	6	6	2
	⎣ Mates and errand-boys .	1	3	6	19
47	Domestic work ⎡ Domestic helps	1	4	15	16
	⎣ Housewives .	7	4	—	—
5	Journalism .	3	—	2	—
17	Armed Forces ⎡ Conscripts .	—	2	9	1
	⎣ N.C.O.s and Officers	—	3	2	—
5	Fishermen .	2	1	—	2
24	Agriculture .	2	3	11	8
17	Other occupations .	—	4	10	3
33	Unemployed .	10	2	12	9
541		75	98	218	150

(After Hermann 1959)

added the subsequent careers of 5 other boys who had been originally rated as mildly dyslexic, the list would have included 3 more research scientists (one a college professor and one a college instructor), one upper- and one middle-management businessman. As the author herself stated: "Of course this (follow-up study) by no means proves, or even suggests, that *all* dyslexics are *good* academic and occupational risks, but the evidence clearly shows that dyslexics cannot be judged to be *poor* risks on the basis of language disability alone; this should be considered when prognoses are being made. Advice to keep the educational and occupational sights very modest would have been inappropriate for most of the boys . . .".

*   *   *

In concluding this present study on "the dyslexic child" I cannot do better than quote the words of Mrs. Margaret Rawson, past President of the Orton Society, when she wrote . . . "if this work generates the optimism which it seems to justify, then clinicians, teachers, parents, and especially the present-day young dyslexic patients or students should feel both more hopeful and more eager to tackle the problems of specific language disability".

There is no justification for anything less than optimism provided only that dyslexics are correctly diagnosed at an early age, and are granted without delay the services of special remedial teaching at the hands of sympathetic experts.

Bibliography

The literature of reading retardation, dyslexia, and learning disorders is now considerable. Since 1964, when *Developmental Dyslexia* was published, the bibliography has been augmented to such an extent that to draw up a complete list of references is almost an impossible task. Early last year it was estimated that more than 20,000 papers had already been published upon this topic. Interested students might with advantage study such periodicals as the *Bulletin of the Word Blind Centre*, the *Bulletin of the Orton Society*, and the *Journal of Learning Disabilities*. The following references are important contributions, and not all of them are necessarily referred to in the text. Some of these monographs and papers are enriched by a considerable number of references to the literature, and these are indicated by an asterisk *.

*de Ajuriaguerra *et al.* (A team from the Geneva Medico-Educational Service) (1968), Problems Posed by Dyslexia, *J. Learning Disab.*, **1**, 158–170. (Full bibliography available on request to the Editorial Office.)

Anzai, E. Iwata, Ikeda (1966), Lese- und Schreibstörungen bei einem 6 Jähringen Knaben, *Psych. Neurol. Jap.*, **68**, 629–640.

Arajärvi, T., Louhivuori, K., Hagman, H., Syvälahti, R., Hietanen, A. (1965), The Role of Specific Reading and Writing Difficulties in Various School Problems, *Ann. Paediat. Fenn.*, **11**, 138–147.

Asso, D., Wyke, M. (1967), Experimental Study of the Effect of Letter Reversals in Reading, *Brit. J. Psychol.*, **58**, 413–419.

Boder, E. (1968), Developmental Dyslexia: A Diagnostic Screening Procedure based on Three Characteristic Patterns of Reading and Spelling, *Claremont Reading Conf. 32nd Yearbook*.

Cole, M., Kraft, M. B. (1964), Specific Learning Disability, *Cortex*, **1**, 302–313.

Critchley, E. M. R. (1968), Reading Retardation, Dyslexia and Delinquency, *Brit. J. Psych.*, **114**, 1537–1547.

Critchley, M. (1966), The Enigma of Gerstmann's Syndrome, *Brain*, **89**, 183–198.

Critchley, M. (1966), Is Developmental Dyslexia the Expression of Minor Cerebral Damage? Wm. Copeland Mem. Lect. Washington D.C., March 26th, 1966. *The Slow Learning Child*, **13**, 9–19.

Critchley, M. (1967), Observations on Developmental Dyslexia. In Modern Trends in Neurology. D. Williams (Ed.), London: Butterworth & Co., p. 135.

Critchley, M. (1968), Developmental Dyslexia, *Paediat. Clin. N. Amer.*, **15**, 669–676.

Critchley, M., Specific Developmental Dyslexia, **14**, 165–173.

Critchley, M. (1969), Specific Developmental Dyslexia, *Brit. J. Hosp. Med.*, 910–911.

*Crosby, R. M. N., with Liston, R. A. (1969), Reading and the Dyslexic Child, Souvenir Press, London.

*Debray, P. *et al.* (1968), La Dyslexie de L'enfant, *Gaz. Méd. de France*, **75**, 5181– Issue devoted to papers on this topic.

Doehring, Dr. G. (Ed.) (1968), Patterns of Impairment in Specific Reading Disability (a Neuropsychological investigation), Indiana Univ. Press, Bloomington, Ind.

Faglioni, P., Gatti, B., Paganoni, A. M., Robutti, A. (1967), La valutazione psicometrica della dislessia, *Infanzia Anormale*, **81**, 628–661.

Flower, R. M., Gofman, H. F., Lawson, L. I. (Edits.) (1963), Reading Disorders. A Multi-disciplinary Symposium, F. A. Davis Company, Philadelphia.

Gatti, B., Paganoni, A. M., Robutti, A. (1968), Influenza dei fattori socioculturali sull'apprendimento del linguaggio scritto, *Infanzia Anormale*, **91**, 718–736.

de Hirsch, K., Jansky, J. J., Langford, W. S., The Prediction of Reading, Spelling and Writing Disabilities in Children, Columbia Univ. Contract U-1270. Final report to the Health Research Council of the City of New York. No date.

*Keeney, A. H., Keeney, V. T. (Edits.) (1968), *Dyslexia*, C. V. Mosley Company, St. Louis.

Lecours, A. R. (1966), Serial Order in Writing—A Study of Mis-spelled Words in Developmental Dysgraphia, *Neuropsychol.*, **4**, 221–241.

*Lesèvre, N. (1964), *Les mouvements oculaires d'exploration*, Thèse de Paris.

Limbosch, N., Luminet-Jasinski, A., Dierkens-Dopchie, N. (1968), *La Dyslexie à l'école primaire*, Ed. de l'Institut de Sociologie, Univ. Libre de Bruxelles.

Lovell, K., Shapton, Dr., Warren, N. S. (1964), A Study of Some Cognitive and other Disabilities in Backward Readers of Average Intelligence as Assessed by a Non-Verbal Test, *Brit. J. Educ. Psychol.*, **34**, 58–64.

Makita, K. (1968), The Rarity of Reading Disability in Japanese Children, *Am. J. Orthopsych.*, **38**, 599–614.

*Mattlinger, M. J. (*née* Lemonnier), (1967), *Donneés statistiques sur la Dyslexie de l'enfant*. Thèse de Paris, Editions A.G.E.M.P., Paris.

Morris, J. M. (1966), *Standards and Progress in Reading*, Nat. Found. Educ. Res. Engl. Wales, Research Reports, Second Series, No. 1.

Obi, I. (1957), Ueber die angeborene Lese- und Schreibscwäche, *Psych. Neurol. Jap.*, **59**, 852–867.

Oettinger, L. Jnr., Cerebral Dysrhythmia induced by Reading. Subclinical Reading Epilepsy, Internat. Copenhagen Congr. Sci. Study. Ment. Retard, August 7th–14th, 1964, No. 58, 460–465.

Oettinger, L. Jnr., The Use of Drugs in Children with Learning Disorders, Internat. Copenhagen Congr. Sci. Study Ment. Retard., August 7th–14th, 1964, No. 16, 256–259.

Oettinger, L. Jnr., Nekonishi, H., Gill, I. G. (1967), Cerebral Dysrhythmia induced by Reading (Subclinical Reading Epilepsy), *Dec. Med. Child Neur.*, **9**, 191–201.

Poeck, K., Orgass, B. (1969), An Experimental Investigation of Finger Agnosia, *Neurology*, **19**, 801–807.

de Quiros, J. B. (1964), Dysphasia and Dyslexia in School Children, *Folia Phoniat.*, **16**, 201–222.

de Quiros, J. B., Della Cella, M. (1965), La Dislexia en la Niñez, Edit. Paidos, Buenos Aires.

de Quiros, J. B., Della Cella, M., Carrara, D., Allegro, L. (1962), Investigaciones sobre la Disfasia Escolar, *Fonoaudiológica*, **8**, 22–68.

de Quiros, J. B., Della Cella, M., Carrara, D., Allegro, L. (1962), Estudios sobre la Dislexia Infantil, Prov. Santa Fe, Ministerio de Educacion y Cultura, Repub. Argentina.

*Rawson, M. B. (1966), A Bibliography on the Nature, Recognition and Treatment of Language Difficulties, Prepared for the Orton Soc. Inc., U.S.A.

Rawson, M. B. (1968), *Developmental Language Disability*, Johns Hopkins Press, Baltimore.

Silver, A., Hagin, R. A. (1964), Specific Reading Disability: Follow-up Studies, *Amer. J. Orthopsych.*, **34**, 95.

Shankweiler, D. (1964), Developmental Dyslexia: A Critique and Review of Recent Evidence, *Cortex*, **1**, 53–62.

Taft, L. T., Cohen, H. J. (1968), Aetiologies of Dyslexia, *Bull. N.Y. Acad. Med.*, **44**, 478–487.

*Thompson, J. L. (1966), *Reading Disability*, Charles C. Thomas, Springfield, Ill.

Tomatis, A. (1967), *La Dyslexie*, Organisation des Centres du Langage, Paris.

Åberg, A. (1958), *Karl XI*, Wahlstrom & Widstrand, Stockholm.

Alajouanine, Th., Lhermitte, F., de Ribaucourt-Ducarne, B. (1960), Les Alexies agnosiques et aphasiques, in *Les Grandes Activités du Lobe Occipital*, Paris, Masson, p. 235.

Altus, G. T. (1956), A WISC Profile for Retarded Readers, *J. Consult. Psychol.*, **20**, 155–156.

Anderson, C. J., Merton, E. (1920), Remedial Work in Reading, *Elem. School J.*, **20**, 685–701, 772–791.

124   *The dyslexic child*

Anderson, I. H., Dearborn, W. F. (1952), *The Psychology of Teaching Reading*, New York, Ronald Press.
Anderson, M., Kelley, M. (1931), An Inquiry into Traits Associated with Reading Disability, *Smith College Stud. in Social Work*, **2**, 46–63.
Arthur, G. (1940), Therapy with Retarded Readers, *J. Consult. Psychol.*, **4**, 173–176.
Axline, V. M. (1947), Non-directive Therapy for Poor Readers, *J. Consult. Psychol.*, **11**, 61–69.
Bachmann, F. (1927), Uber kongenitale Wortblindheit (angeborene Leseschwäche), *Abhandl. Neur. Psych. Psychol. Grenzgeb.*, **40**, 1–72.
Bakwin, H. (1950), Psychiatric Aspects of Pediatrics: Lateral Dominance, Right- and Left-handedness, *J. Pediat.*, **36**, 385–391.
Barger, W. C., Lavin, R., Speight, F. S. (1957), Constitutional Psychiatry of Poor Readers, *Dis. Nerv. Sys.*, **18**, 289–294.
Bastian, H. C. (1898), *A Treatise on Aphasia and Other Speech Defects*, London, Lewis.
Bateman, F. (1890), *On Aphasia or Loss of Speech*, 2nd Ed., London, J. & A. Churchill.
Bender, L. (1956), Problems in Conceptualisation and Communication in Children with Development Alexia, *Proc. Amer. Psychobiol. Ass.*
Bender, L. (1956), Research Studies from Bellevue Hospital on Specific Reading Disabilities, *Bull. Orton Soc.*, **6**, 1–3.
Bender, L. (1957), Specific Reading Disability as a Maturational Lag, *Bull. Orton Soc.*, **7**, 9–18.
Bender, L. (1959), Report on Dyslexia—International Congress of Child Psychiatry, *Bull. Orton Soc.*, **9**, 26.
Bender, L., Schilder, P. (1951), Graphic Art as a Special Ability in Children with a Reading Disability, *J. clin. exp. Psychopath.*, **12**, 147–156.
Bennett, C. C. (1938), An Inquiry into the Genesis of Poor Reading, *Contrib. Educ. No. 755, Bureau Publ., Teaching Col., Columbus Univ.*
Benton, A. L. (1958), Significance of Systematic Reversal in Right-left Discrimination, *Acta Psych. Neur. Scand.*, **33**, 129–137.
Benton, A. L. (1959), *Right-left Discrimination and Finger-localisation: Development and Pathology*, New York, Paul C. Hoeber.
Benton, A. L. (1962), Dyslexia in Relation to Form Perception and Directional Sense, Chap. VI of *Reading Disability. Progress and Research Needs in Dyslexia*, edit. J. Money. Baltimore, John Hopkins Press.
Benton, A. L., Kemble, J. D. (1960), Right-left Orientation and Reading Disability, *Psych. & Neur.*, **139**, 49–60.
Berkhan, O. (1885), Uber die Störung der Schriftsprache bei Halbidioten und ihre Ähnlichkeit mit den Stammeln, *Arch. f. Psych.*, **16**, 78–86.
Berkhan, O. (1917), Uber die Wortblindheit ein Stammeln im Sprechen und Schreiben, ein Fehl im Lesen, *Neurol. Centralbl.*, **36**, 914–927.
Berlin, R. (1887), *Eine besondere Art der Wortblindheit (Dyslexia)*, Wiesbaden.
Betts, E. A. (1936), *The Prevention and Correction of Reading Difficulties*, San Francisco, Row.
Betts, E. A. (1950), *Foundations of Reading Instruction with Emphasis on Differentiated Guidance*, Amer. Book Co.
Birch, H. G. (1962), Dyslexia and the Maturation of Visual Function, Chap. X of *Reading Disability. Progress and Research Needs in Dyslexia*, edit. J. Money. Baltimore, John Hopkins Press.
Bjork, A. (1955), The Electromyogram of the Extraocular Muscles in Opticokinetic Nystagmus and in Reading, *Acta Ophth.*, **33**, 437–454.
Bladergroen, W. J. (1955), Uber die Diagnostik und Therapie von Lesehemmungen, *Prax. Kinderpsychol.*, **4**, 6–14.
Blanchard, P. (1936), Reading Disabilities in Relation to Difficulties of Personality and Emotional Development, *Ment. Hyg.*, **20**, 384–413.
Blanchard, P. (1946), Psychoanalytic Contributions to the Problems of Reading Disabilities, *Psychoanal. Stud. Child.*, **2**, 163–188.
Blom, E. C. (1928), Mirror Writing, *Psychol. Bull.*, **25**, 582–594.
Bond, G. L., Tinker, M. A. (1957), *Reading Difficulties, their Diagnosis and Correction*, New York, Appleton-Century-Crofts.

Borel-Maisonny, S. (1956), Dyslexie et dysorthographie, *Rev. franç. hyg. med. schol. univ.*, **9**, 15–24.
Boyce, E. R. (1949), *Learning to Read*, London, Macmillan.
Broadbent, W. (1872), Cerebral Mechanisms of Speech and Thought, *Trans. Roy. Med. Chir. Soc.*, **55**, 145–194.
Broadbent, W. (1896), Note on Dr. Hinshelwood's Communication on Word-blindness and Visual Memory, *Lancet*, **1**, 18.
Bronner, A. F. (1917), *The Psychology of Special Abilities and Disabilities*, Boston, Little, Brown & Co.
Burt, C. (1950), *The Backward Child*, 3rd Edit., London, Univ. Lond. Press.
Burt, C. (1960), The Readability of Type, *New Scientist*, **7**, 277–279.
Buswell, G. T. (1947), The Sub-vocalisation Factor in the Improvement of Reading, *Elem. School J.*, **48**, 190–196.
Carnvale, E. (1961), The Etiology of Reading Disability, *Lab. Rep. No. 2, Comm. Proj. Sect., Ment. Health Study Center.*
Carter, D. B. (1953), A Further Demonstration of Phi Movement in Cerebral Dominance, *J. Psychol.*, **36**, 299–309.
Carter, H. J. L. (1930), Disabilities in Reading, *Elem. School. J.*, **31**, 120–132.
Center, B. (1954), Perceptual Function in Reading Problems, *Optom. Weekly*, **45**, 311–312.
Chesni, Y. (1959), Retard de langage chez l'enfant. Recherche statistique sur la dyslexie specifique en relation avec les troubles de la dominance laterale et de l'orientation spatio-temporale, *Rev. neur.*, **101**, 576–582.
Childs, S. B. (1959), The Teaching of Reading Abroad, *Bull. Orton Soc.*, **9**, 19–25.
Claiborne, J. H. (1906), Types of Congenital Symbol Amblyopia, *J. Amer. Med. Ass.* **47**, 1813–1816.
Claparède (1916), Bradylexie bei einem sonst normalen Kinde, XI Meeting Swiss Neurol. Soc., May 13 and 14, *Abs. Neur. Zlbl.*, 1917, **36**, 572.
Clark, B. (1935), The Effect of Binocular Imbalance on the Behaviour of the Eyes During Reading, *J. Educ. Psychol.*, **26**, 530–538.
Clark, B. (1940), Binocular Anomalies and Reading Ability, *Am. J. Oph.*, **23**, 885–891.
Cohn, R. (1961), Delayed Acquisition of Reading and Writing Abilities in Children: a Neurological Study, *Arch. neur.*, **4**, 153–164.
Cole, E. M. (1942), The Neurologic Aspects of Defects in Speech and Reading, *New Eng. J. Med.*, **226**, 977–980.
Comfort, F. D. (1931), Lateral Dominance and Reading Disability, *Am. Psychol. Assoc.*, Sept. 11, 1931, Toronto.
Creak, M. (1936), Reading Difficulties in Children, II, *Arch. Dis. Child.*, 143–156
Critchley, M. (1927), *Mirror Writing*, London, Kegan Paul.
Crtichley, M. (1927), Some Defects of Reading and Writing in Children: Their Association with Word-blindness and Mirror-writing, *J. State med.*, **35**, 217–223.
Critchley, M. (1942), Aphasic Disorders of Signalling (Constitutional and Acquired) Occurring in Naval Signalmen, *J. Mount Sinai Hosp.*, **9**, 363–375.
Critchley, M. (1953), *The Parietal Lobes*, London, Arnold.
Critchley, M. (1961), Doyne Memorial Lecture, Inborn Reading Disorders of Central Origin, *Tr. Oph. Soc.*, **81**, 459–480.
Critchley, M. (1962), Developmental Dyslexia: a Constitutional Dyssymbolia, in *Word-blindness or Specific Developmental Dyslexia*, edit. A. W. Franklin. London, Pitman Med. Publ. Co. Ltd., pp. 45–48.
Critchley, M. (1963), The Problem of Developmental Dyslexia, *Proc. Roy. Soc. Med.*, **56**, 209–212.
Currier, F. P., Jr., Dewar, M. (1927), Word-blindness: Difficulty in Reading in School-children, *J. Mich. Med. Soc.*, **26**, 300–304.
Dale, N. (1902), *Further Notes on the Teaching of English Reading*, London and Liverpool, Philip & Son.
Daniels, J. C. (1962), Reading Difficulty and Aural Training, in *Word-blindness or Specific Developmental Dyslexia*, edit. A. W. Franklin. London, Pitman Med. Publ. Co. Ltd., pp. 87–92.
Daniels, J. C., Diack, H. (1956), *Progress in Reading*, Univ. Nottingham Inst. Educ.
Dearborn, W. F. (1931), Ocular and Manual Dominance in Dyslexia, Paper read before Amer. Psychol. Ass., Sept. 11, 1931, Toronto.

Dearborn, W. F. (1933), Structural Factors which Condition Special Disability in Reading, *Proc. 57th Ann. Sess., Amer. Ass. Ment. Def.*, p. 268.
Dearborn, W. F., Leverett, H. M. (1945), Visual Defects and Reading, *J. exp. Educ.*, **13**, 111–124.
Dejerine, J. (1892), Contribution à l'étude anatomo-pathologique et clinique des différents variétés de cecité verbale, *Comp. rend. scéan. soc. biol.*, sér. 9, **4**, 61–90.
Delacato, C. H. (1959), *The Treatment and Prevention of Reading Problems*, Springfield, Ill., C. C. Thomas.
Diack, Hunter (1960), *Reading and the Psychology of Perception*, Nottingham, Peter Skinner Publishing Ltd.
Dolch, E. W. (1948), *Problems in Reading*, Garrard Press.
Dosužkov, B. (1961), Vztak motorické a sensorické laterality u leváku, *Čžl. Neur.*, **24**, 136–143.
Downey, J. E. (1927), Types of Dextrality and their Implications, *Amer. J. Psychol.*, **38**, 317–367.
Drew, A. L. (1956), A Neurological Appraisal of Familial Congenital Word-blindness, *Brain*, **79**, 440–460.
Duche, J. (1958), Les dyslexies, *Rev. franç hyg. ment. scol.*, **11**, 129–138.
Dugas, M. (1956), Dyslexies et dysorthographies, *Presse méd.*, **64**, 1435–1438.
Duguid, K. (1935), Congenital Word-blindness and Reading Disability, *Guy's Hosp. Rep.*, **85**, 76–93.
Duncan, J. (1953), *Backwardness in Reading: Remedies and Prevention*, London, Harrap.
Durbrow, H. C. (1952), Teaching the Strephosymbolic. 1. At the Primary Level, *Bull. Orton Soc.*, **2**, 7–9.
Eames, T. H. (1932), A Comparison of the Ocular Characteristics of Unselected and Reading Disability Groups, *J. Educ. res.*, **25**, 211–215.
Eames, T. H. (1934), Low Fusion Convergence as a Factor in Reading Disability, *Am. J. Oph.*, **17**, 709–710.
Eames, T. H. (1935), A Frequency Study of Physical Handicaps in Reading Disability and Unselected Groups, *J. Educ. res.*, **29**, 1–5.
Eames, T. H. (1938), The Ocular Conditions of 350 Poor Readers, *J. Educ. res.*, **32**, 10–16.
Eames, T. H. (1944), Amblyopia in Cases of Reading Failure, *Am. J. Oph.*, **27**, 1374–1375.
Eames, T. H. (1945), Comparison of Children of Premature and Full-term Birth who Fail in Reading, *J. Educ. res.*, **38**, 506–508.
Eames, T. H. (1948), Incidence of Diseases Among Reading Failures and Non-failures, *J. Pediat.*, **33**, 614–617.
Eames, T. H. (1948), Comparison of Eye Conditions Among 1,000 Reading Failures, 500 Ophthalmic Patients, and 150 Unselected Children, *Am. J. Oph.*, **31**, 713–717.
Eames, T. H. (1955), The Relationship of Birth Weight, the Speeds of Object and Word Perception, and Visual Acuity, *J. Pediat.*, **47**, 603–606.
Edfeldt, A. W. (1959), *Silent Speech and Silent Reading*, Stockholm, Almqvist & Wiksell.
Ellis, A. (1949), Results of a Mental Hygiene Approach to Reading Disability Problems, *J. Consult. psychol.*, **13**, 56–61.
Engler, B. (1917), Über Analphabetia Partialis: (kongenitale Wortblindheit), *Monat. Psych. Neur.*, **42**, 119–132.
Ettlinger, G., Jackson, C. V. (1955), Organic Factors in Developmental Dyslexia, *Proc. Roy. Soc., Med.*, **48**, 998–1000.
Eustis, R. S. (1947), The Primary Etiology of the Specific Language Disabilities, *J. Pediat.*, **31**, 448–455.
Eustis, R. S. (1947), Specific Reading Disability, *New Engl. J. Med.*, **237**, 243–249.
Ewart, E. (1955), A Reading Disability Analysed: Word-blindness, *The Schoolmaster*, 1073–1074.
Fabian, A. A. (1945), Vertical Rotation in Visual Motor Performance; its Relationship to Reading Reversals, *J. Educ. Psychol.*, **36**, 129–145.
Faust, C. (1954), Hirnpathologische Studie zur kongenitalen Schreib-Lese-Schwäche *Nervenarzt.*, **25**, 137–145.

Fernald, G. (1943), *On Certain Language Disabilities: Nature and Treatment*, Baltimore, Williams & Wilkins.

Fernald, G., Keller, H. (1921), The Effect of Kinæsthetic Factors in the Development of Word-recognition in Non-readers, *J. Educ. res.*, **4**, 355–377.

Feyeux, A. (1932), *L'Acquisition du Langage et ses Retards*, Paris, Editions Médicales N. Maloine.

Filbin, R. L. (1957), Prescription for the Johnny Who Can't Read, *Elementary English*, **34**, 559–561.

Fildes, L. G. (1921), A Psychological Inquiry into the Nature of the Condition Known as Congenital Word-blindness, *Brain*, **44**, 286–307.

Fisher, J. H. (1905), A Case of Congenital Word-blindness (Inability to Learn to Read), *Oph. Rev.*, **24**, 315–318.

Fisher, J. H. (1910), Congenital Word-blindness (Inability to Learn to Read), *Trans. Oph. Soc. U.K.*, **30**, 216–225.

Flesch, R. (1955), *Why Johnny Can't Read*, New York, Harper.

Foerster, R. (1904), A propos de la Pathologie de la Lecture et de l'Ecriture (cécité verbale congénitale chez un débile), *Rev. neur.*, **12**, 200–202.

Forgays, D. G. (1953), The Development of Differential Word Recognition, *J. exp. Psychol.*, **45**, 165–168.

Frank, H. (1936), "Word-blindness" in School-children, *Trans. Oph. Soc. U.K.*, **56**, 231–238.

Frank, H. (1935), A Comparative Study of Children who are Backward in Reading and Beginners in the Infant School, *Brit. J. Educ. psychol.*, **5**, 41–58.

Franklin, A. W. (1962), Ed. *Word-blindness or Specific Developmental Dyslexia*, London, Pitman Med. Publ. Co. Ltd.

Franstrom, K. O. (1958), Difficulties in Reading and Writing (Word Blindness). III. Ophthalmological Aspects. *Nord. med.*, **59**, 518–519.

Freeman, F. N. (1916), Experiments with School-subjects: Observations of Eye-movements in Reading, *Experimental Education*, pp. 95–109, Houghton Mifflin Co.

Freeman, J. D. J. (1957), Reading Difficulties in Childhood, *Trans. oph. soc. U.K.*, **77**, 611–613.

Freud, S. (1953), *On Aphasia*, London, Imago Publ. Co. Trans. by E. Stengel. (Originally published 1891.)

Gallagher, J. R. (1960), Specific Language Disability: Dyslexia, *Bull. Orton Soc.*, **10**, 5–10.

Gallagher, J. R. (1962), Word-blindness (Reading-disability; Dyslexia): Its Diagnosis and Treatment, in *Word-blindness or Specific Developmental Dyslexia*, edit. E. W. Franklin. London, Pitman Med. Publ. Co. Ltd., pp. 6–14.

Gann, E. (1945), *Reading Difficulty and Personality Organisation*, New York, Kings Crown Press, Columbia Univ.

Gates, A. I. (1922), The Psychology of Reading and Spelling with Special Reference to Disability, *Teachers Coll. Contrib. Educ. No. 129.* Teachers Coll., Columbia Univ.

Gates, A. I., Bond, G. L. (1936), Reading Readiness. A Study of Factors Determining Success and Failure in Beginning Reading, *Teach. Coll. Rec.*, **37**, 679–685.

Gates, A. I. (1937), Diagnosis and Treatment of Extreme Cases of Reading Disability, *Nat. Soc. Stud. Educ. Yearbook*, 36 (1), 391, Chicago.

Gates, A. I. (1941), The Role of Personality Maladjustment in Reading Disability, *J. genet. psych.*, **59**, 77–83.

Gates, A. I., Bond, G. L. (1936), Relation of Handedness, Eye-sighting and Acuity Dominance to Reading, *J. Educ. psychol.*, **27**, 450–456.

Geiger, R. (1923), A Study in Reading Diagnosis, *J. Educ. Res.*, **8**, 282–300.

Gellerman, S. W. (1949), Causal Factors in the Reading Difficulties of Elementary School-children, *Elem. School J.*, **49**, 523–530.

Gillingham, A. (1956), The Prevention of Scholastic Failure Due to Specific Language Disability, *Bull. Orton Soc.*, **6**, 26–31.

Gillingham, A., Stillman, B. U. (1956), *Remedial Training for Children with Specific Disability in Reading, Spelling, and Penmanship* (5th Edit.), New York, Sackett and Wilhelms Litho. Corp.

Gjessing, H. J. (1958), Reading Difficulties in Children, *T. norske Laegef.*, **78**, 187–191.

Goetzinger, C. P., Dirks, D. D., Baer, C. J. (1960), Auditory Discrimination and
  Visual Perception in Good and Poor Readers, *Ann. Otol. Rhin. Laryng.*, **69**,
  121–136.
Goins, J. T. (1958), Visual Perceptual Abilities and Early Reading Progress,
  Suppl. Educ. Monogr. No. 87, Chicago.
Goldberg, H. K. (1959), The Ophthalmologist Looks at the Reading Problem,
  Am. J. Oph., **47**, 67–74.
Goldberg, H. K., Marshall, C., Simms, E. (1960), The Role of Brain Damage in
  Congenital Dyslexia, *Am. J. Oph.*, **50**, 586–590.
Gooddy, W. (1963), Directional Features of Reading and Writing, *Proc. Roy. Soc.
  Med.*, **56**, 206–212.
Gooddy, W., Reinhold, M. (1961), Congenital Dyslexia and Asymmetry of Cerebral
  Function, *Brain*, **84**, 231–242.
Granjon-Galifret, N., Ajuriaguerra, J. (1951), Troubles de l'apprentissage de la
  lecture et dominance latérale, *Encéphale*, **40**, 385–398.
Granstrom, K. O., Åberg, A. (1961), Kunglig ordblindhet. Karl XI's läsochskriv-
  svårigheter, *Svenska Lakertidn.*, **58**, 915–927.
Gray, W. S. (1921), Diagnostic and Remedial Steps in Reading, *J. Educ. res.*, **4**,
  1–15.
Gray, W. S. (1912), *Remedial Cases in Reading: Their Diagnosis and Treatment*,
  Suppl. Educ. Monogr. No. 22, Depart. Educ., Chicago Univ., Chicago Press.
Gray, W. S. (1956), *Teaching of Reading and Writing: An International Survey*,
  UNESCO monogr., Evans Bros. Ltd., London.
Grewel, F. (1958), Ontwikkelingsdyslexie (Leeszwakte), *Nederl. Tijd. Geneesk.*,
  102, 183–190.
Gruber, E. (1962), Reading Ability, Binocular Coordination and the Ophthalmo-
  graph, *Arch. Oph.*, **67**, 280–288.
Günther, M. (1928), Beitrage zur Psycho-pathologie und Klinik der sogennanten
  kongenitalen Leseschwäche, *Ztschr. kinderforsch.*, **34**, 585.
Hall, R., Word-blindness: its Cause and Cure.
Hallgren, B. (1950), Specific Dyslexia, *Acta psych. neur.*, Suppl. No. 65, 1–287.
Hallgren, B. (1952), Specifik Dyslexi, *Socialmed. Tidskr.*, **29**, 70–78.
Hambright, H. (1956), The Prevention of Scholastic Failure Due to Specific Language
  Disability, *Bull. Orton Soc.*, **6**, 32–36.
Hardy, W. G. (1962), Dyslexia in Relation to Diagnostic Methodology in Hearing
  and Speech Disorders, in *Reading Disability*, edit. J. Money. Baltimore, John
  Hopkins Press.
Harris, A. J. (1957), Lateral Dominance, Directional Confusion and Reading
  Disability, *J. Psychol.*, **44**, 283–294.
Harris, A. J., Roswell, F. G. (1953), Clinical Diagnosis of Reading Disability,
  J. Psychol., **36**, 323–340.
Hawthorne, J. W. (1935), The Effect of Improvement in Reading Ability on Intelli-
  gence Test-scores, *J. Educ. Psychol.*, **26**, 41–51.
Heller, T. M. (1963), Word-blindness; a Survey of the Literature and a Report of
  Twenty-eight Cases, *Pediatrics*, **31**, 669–691.
Henry, S. (1947), Children's Audiograms in Relation to Reading Attainments,
  J. genet. Psychol., **70**, 211–231; **71**, 3–48; 49–63.
Hermann, K. (1949), Alexia-agraphia. A Case Report (Acquired Reading and
  Writing Disabilities, Temporary Word-blindness of the Congenital Type), *Acta
  psych. neur.*, **25**, 449–455.
Hermann, K. (1956), Congenital Word-blindness, *Acta Psych. Neur. Scand.*, Suppl.
  108, 117–184.
Hermann, K. (1959), *Reading Disability*, Copenhagen, Munksgaard.
Hermann, K. (1961), Kliniske Iagttagelser und medfødt ordblindhed, *Nord. Tidssk.
  for Tale og Stemme*, **21**, 31–40.
Hermann, K., Norrie, E. (1958), Is Congenital Word-blindness a Hereditary Type of
  Gerstmann's Syndrome? *Psych. Neur.*, **136**, 59–73.
Hermann, K. and Voldby, H. (1946), The Morphology of Handwriting in Congenital
  Word-blindness, *Acta Psych. Neur.*, **21**, 349–363.
Hibbert, F. G. (1961), Dyslexia, Proc. Soc. Brit. Neurosurg., 62nd Meeting at
  Swansea, Nov. 25–26, 1960. Reported in *J. Neur. Neurosurb. Psych.*, 1961, **24**,
  N.S. 93–94.

Hildreth, G., (1936), *Learning the Three Rs*, Minneapolis Educ. Publ., pp. IX and 824.
Hildreth, G. (1945), A School Survey of Eye-hand Dominance, *J. Appl. Psychol.*, **29**, 83–88.
Hilman, H. H. (1956), The Effect of Laterality on Reading Disability, *Durham Res. Rev.*, **7**, 86–96.
Hincks, E. (1926), *Disability in Reading in Relation to Personality*, Harvard Monogr. Educ., Whole No. 7, Ser. 1, Vol. 2, No. 2, Camb. Univ. Press.
Hinshelwood, J. (1895), Word-blindness and Visual Memory, *Lancet*, **2**, 1564–1570.
Hinshelwood, J. (1896), A Case of Dyslexia: a Peculiar Form of Word-blindness, *Lancet*, **2**, 1451–1454.
Hinshelwood, J. (1896), The Visual Memory for Words and Figures, *Brit. med. J.*, **2**, 1543–1544.
Hinshelwood, J. (1898), A Case of "Word" without "Letter" Blindness, *Lancet*, **1**, 422–425.
Hinshelwood, J. (1899), "Letter" without "Word" Blindness, *Lancet*, **1**, 83–86.
Hinshelwood, J. (1900), Congenital Word-blindness, *Lancet*, **1**, 1506–1508.
Hinshelwood, J. (1900). *Letter-, Word- and Mind-blindness*, London, Lewis.
Hinshelwood, J. (1902), Four Cases of Word-blindness, *Lancet*, **1**, 358–363.
Hinshelwood, J. (1902), Congenital Word-blindness, with Reports of Two Cases, *Oph. Rev.*, **21**, 91–99.
Hinshelwood, J. (1904), A Case of Congenital Word-blindness, *Ophthalmoscope*, **2**, 399–405.
Hinshelwood, J. (1904), A Case of Congenital Word-blindness, *Brit. med. J.*, **2**, 1303–1307.
Hinshelwood, J. (1907), Four Cases of Congenital Word-blindness Occurring in the Same Family, *Brit. med. J.*, **2**, 1229.
Hinshelwood, J. (1911), Two Cases of Hereditary Word-blindness, *Brit. med. J.*, **1**, 608.
Hinshelwood, J. (1912), The Treatment of Word-blindness, Acquired and Congenital, *Brit. med. J.*, **2**, 1033–1035.
Hinshelwood, J. (1917), *Congenital Word-blindness*, London, Lewis.
Hirsch, K. de (1957), Tests Designed to Discover Potential Reading Difficulties at the 6-year-old Level, *Amer. J. Orthopsych.*, **27**, 566–576.
Hoffmann, J. (1927), Uber Entwicklung und Stand der Lesepsychologie, *Arch. ges. Psychol.*, **57**, 401–444.
Hoffmann, J. (1927), Experimentalpsychologische Untersuchungen über Leseleistungen von Schulkinden, *Arch. ges. Psychol.*, **58**, 325–388.
Holt, L. M. (1962), The Treatment of Word-blind Children at Saint Bartholomew's, in *Word-blindness or Specific Developmental Dyslexia*, edit. A. W. Franklin. London, Pitman Med. Publ. Co. Ltd., pp. 93–98.
Holt, M. (1963), Children Suffering from Word Blindness, *A.W.B.C. Bulletin*, **1**, 3–4.
Huey, E. B. (1908), *The Psychology and Pegagogy of Reading*, New York, Macmillan Co.
Illing, E. (1929), Uber kongenitale Wortblindheit (angeborene Schreib- und Leseschwäche), *Monat. Psych. Neur.*, **71**, 297–355.
Ingram, T. T. S. (1959), Specific Developmental Disorders of Speech in Childhood, *Brain*, **82**, 450–467.
Ingram, T. T. S. (1959), A Description and Classification of the Common Disorders of Speech in Children, *Arch. Dis. Child.*, **34**, 444.
Ingram, T. T. S. (1960), Pædiatric Aspects of Specific Developmental Dysphasia, Dyslexia and Dysgraphia, *Cerebral Palsy Bull.*, **2**, 254–277.
Ingram, T. T. S. (1963), The Association of Speech Retardation and Educational Difficulties, *Proc. Roy. Soc. Med.*, **56**, 199–203.
Ingram, T. T. S., Reid, J. F. (1956), Developmental Aphasia Observed in a Department of Child Psychiatry, *Arch. Dis. Child.*, **31**, 161–172.
Jackson, E. (1906), Developmental Alexia (Congenital Word-blindness), *Amer. J. med. Sci.*, **131**, 843–849.
Jackson, J. (1944), A Survey of Psychological, Social and Environmental Differences between Advanced and Retarded Readers, *J. genet. Psychol.*, **65**, 113–131.
Jansky, J. J. (1958), A Case of Severe Dyslexia with Aphasic-like Symptoms, *Bull. Orton Soc.*, **8**, 8–10.

Jastak, J. (1934), Interferences in Reading, *Psychol. Bull.*, **31**, 244–272.
Jenkins, D. L., Brown, A. W., Elmendorf, L. (1937), Mixed Dominance and Reading Disability, *Amer. J. Orthopsych.*, **7**, 72–81.
Jones, M. M. W. (1944), Relationship between Reading Deficiencies and Left-handedness, *School & Soc.*, **60**, 238.
Judd, C. H., Buswell, G. T., *Silent Reading: A Study of Various Types*, Suppl. Educ. Monogr., Dept. Educ., Univ. Chicago, No. 23.
Judd, C. H., Gray, W. S., McLaughlin, K., Schmidt, C., Gilliland, A. R. (1918), *Reading: Its Nature and Development*, Supp. Educ. Monogr., Dept. Educ., Univ. Chicago II, No. 4.
Kabersek, V. (1960), *L'Electro-oculographie ou l'enregistrement des mouvements oculaires. Son application à l'etude de la lecture normale et des anomalies pathologiques de la Lecture*, Paris, Foulon.
Kågén, B. (1943), Om ordblindhet, *Pedagog. skrifter.*, **60**, 179–180.
Kawi, A. A., Pasamanick, B. (1958), Association of Factors of Pregnancy with Reading Disorders in Childhood, *J. Amer. Med. Assoc.*, **166**, 1420–1423.
Kawi, A. A., Pasamanick, B. (1959), Prenatal and Paranatal Factors in the Development of Childhood Reading Disorders, *Monogr. Soc. Res. Child. Dev.*, **24**, No. 4, 1–80.
Kennard, M. A., Rabinovitch, R. D., Wexler, D. (1952), The Abnormal Electro-encephalogram as Related to Reading Disability in Children with Disorders of Behavior, *Canad. Med. Ass. J.*, **67**, 330–333.
Kerr, J. (1897), School Hygiene, in its Mental, Moral and Physical Aspects. Howard Medal Prize Essay, *J. Roy. Statist. Soc.*, **60**, 613–680.
Kerr, J. (1900), Four Unusual Cases of Sensory Aphasia, *Lancet*, **1**, 1446.
Kirmsse (1917–18), Die Priorität in der Begriffsbildung "Wortblindheit", *Zeit. Kinderforsch.*
Krabbe, M. J. (1954), Word-blindness and Image Thinking, *Acta psychother.*, **2**, 52–64.
Krise, E. M. (1949), Reversals in Reading: a Problem in Space Perception, *Elem. School J.*, **49**, 278–284.
Krise, E. M. (1952), An Experimental Investigation of Theories of Reversals in Reading, *J. Educ. Psychol.*, **43**, 408–422.
Kurk, M., Steinbaum, M. (1957), Factors in Reading Disability, *Rev. Optom.*, **94**, 25–26.
Kuromaru, S. and Okada, S. (1961), On Developmental Dyslexia in Japan, Paper read at the 7th Internat. Congr. Neurol., Rome.
Lachmann, F. M. (1960), Perceptical-motor Development in Children Retarded in Reading-ability, *J. Consult. Psychol.*, **24**, 427–431.
Langman, M. P. (1960), The Reading Process: a Descriptive, Interdisciplinary Approach, *Genet Psychol. Monogr.*, **62**, 3–40.
Larmande, A., Sutter, J. M. (1954), Dissociation des acuités visuelles et dyslexie spécifique, *Bull. Soc. franç. Ophth.*, **67**, 220–225.
Larsen, C. Å. (1954), Huad er ordblindhed. In: *2 nord. staevne for laesepaedegogen*, p. 73.
Laubenthal, F. (1936), Uber "kongenitale Wortblindheit", zugleich ein Beitrag zur Klinik sog. partieller Schwächsinnsformen und ihrer erblichen Frundlagen, *Zeit. Neur. Psych.*, **156**, 329–360.
Laubenthal, F. (1938), Uber einige Sonderformen des "angeborenen Schwächsinns" (klinischer und erbbiologischer Beitrag zur Kenntnis der kongenitalen Wortblindheit und Worttaubheit, der Hörstörungen bei Schwächsinnigen und der xeroder mischen Idiotie), *Zeit. Neur. Psych.*, **163**, 233–288.
Laubenthal, F. (1941), Zur Erbhygienischen Bewertung der kongenitalen Wortblindheit, *Der Erbarzt.*, **9**, 156.
Launay, C. (1952), Etude d'une classe d'enfants de 6 à 7 ans inaptes à la lecture, *Sem. Hôp. Paris*, **28**, 1459–1463.
Launay, C. (1952), Etude d'ensemble des inaptitudes à la lecture, *Sem. Hôp. Paris*, **28**, 1463–1474.
Launay, C., Borel-Maisonny, S. (1952), Un cas de "dyslexie spécifique", *Sem. Hôp. Paris*, **28**, 1455–1459.
Lefevre, C. A. (1961), Reading Instruction Related to Primary Language Learning: a Linguistic View, *J. devel. Reading*, **4**, 147–158.

Lewis, H. W., Jr. (1961), A Study of Reading Levels: Standardised Tests and In-formal Tests, The Reading Clinic, Publ. Schools Dist., Columbia.

Ley, A. (1938), Sur l'alexie d'évolution familiale et héréditaire, *Ann. med.-psychol.* **96,** (II), 145–150.

Ley, J., Tordeur, G. W. (1936), Alexie et agraphie d'évolution chez des jumeaux monozygotiques, *J. belge neur. psych.,* **36,** 203–222.

Liessens, P. (1949), L'alexie chez les enfants arriérés, *Acta neur. psych. belg.,* **49,** 102–112.

Looft, C. (1939), Dyslexi og dysgrafi hos skolebarn, *Nord. med.,* **3,** 2621–2626.

Lord, E. E., Carmichael, L., Dearborn, W. F. (1925), *Special Disabilities in Learning to Read and Write,* Harv. Monogr. Educ., Whole No. 6, Ser. 1, Vol. 2, No. 1, Camb. Univ. Press.

Lynn, R. (1955), Personality Factors in Reading Achievement, *Proc. Roy. Soc. Med.,* **48,** 996–997.

Lynn, R. (1957), Temperamental Characteristics Related to Disparity of Attainment in Reading and Arithmetic, *Brit. J. educ. Psychol.,* **27,** 62–67.

Mach, L. (1937), Lese-und Schreibschwäche bei normalbegabten Kindern, *Zeit. Kinderforsch.,* **46,** 113–197.

Macmeeken, A. M. (1939), *The Intelligence of a Representative Group of Scottish Children,* London, Univ. Lond. Press.

Macmeeken, A. M. (1939), *Ocular Dominance in Relation to Developmental Aphasia,* London, Univ. Lond. Press.

Malmquist, E. (1958), *Factors Relating to Reading Disabilities in the First Grade,* Stockholm, Almqvist & Wiksell.

Margolin, J. B., Roman, M., Harari, C. (1955), Reading Disability in the Delin-quent Child: a Microcosm of Psychological Pathology, *Am. J. Orthopsych.,* **25,** 25–35.

Mark, H. J., Hardy, W. G. (1958), Orienting Reflex Disturbances in Central Auditory or Language Handicapped Children, *J. Speech Hear. Dis.,* **23,** 237–242.

Marshall, W., Ferguson, J. H. (1939), Hereditary Word-blindness as a Defect of Selective Association, *J. Nerv. Ment. Dis.,* **89,** 164–173.

Maruyama, M. (1958), Reading Disability: a Neurological Point of View, *Bull. Orton Soc.,* **8,** 14–16.

Mayer, K. (1928), Uber kongenitale Wortblindheit, *Monat. Psych. Neur.,* **70,** 161–177.

McCready, E. B. (1909–10), Congenital Word-blindness as a Cause of Backward-ness in School-children: Report of a Case Associated with Stuttering, *Penn. med. J.,* **13,** 278–284.

McCready, E. B. (1926–27), Defects in the Zone of Language (Word-deafness and Word-blindness) and their Influence in Education and Behaviour, *Am. J. Psych.,* **6** (O.S. **83**), 267–277.

Meredith, C. P. (1963), The Association for Word Blind Children, *A.W.B.C. Bulletin,* **1,** 1–2.

Meredith, P. (1962), Psycho-physical Aspects of Word-blindness and Kindred Disorders, in *Word-blindness or Specific Developmental Dyslexia,* ed. A. W. Franklin. London, Pitman Med. Publ. Co. Ltd., pp. 28–40.

Meyer, H. (1937), Laesevanskeligheder Los Børn (Ordblindhed), *Vor Ungdom.,* **59,** 253.

Miles, T. R. (1962), A Suggested Method of Treatment for Specific Dyslexia, in *Word-blindness or Specific Developmental Dyslexia,* ed. A. W. Franklin. London, Pitman Med. Publ. Co. Ltd., pp. 99–104.

Miles, T. R. (1963), Comments on the Report on "Dyslexia" published in the *Health of the School Child,* 1962. *A.W.B.C. Bulletin,* **1,** 2–3.

Miller, A. D., Margolin, J. B., Yolles, B. F. (1957), Epidemiology of Reading Disabilities: Some Methodologic Considerations and Early Findings, *Amer. J. Publ. Health,* **47,** 1250–1256.

Ministry of Education (1956), Pamphlet No. 30, *Education of the Handicapped Pupil* 1945–1955, London, H.M.S.O., p. 26. (Reprinted 1960.)

Ministry of Education (1957), Pamphlet No. 32, *Standards of Reading* 1948–1956, London, H.M.S.O., p. 46.

Ministry of Education (1962), *The Health of the School Child,* London, H.M.S.O., p. 248.

Money, J. (1962), Ed. *Reading Disability. Progress and Research Needs in Dyslexia*, Baltimore, Johns Hopkins Press.

Monroe, M. (1932), *Children Who Cannot Read*, Chicago, Univ. Chicago Press.

Monroe, M., Backus, B. (1937), *Remedial Reading*, Boston, Houghton Mifflin.

Moor, L. (1961), L'examen psychologique chez les dyslexiques et les dysorthographiques, *Med. Infant.*, **68**, 43–47.

Morgan, D. H. (1939), Twin Similarities in Photographic Measures of Eye-movements while Reading Prose, *J. Educ. Psychol.*, **30**, 572–586.

Morgan, W. Pringle (1896), A Case of Congenital Word-blindness, *Brit. med. J.*, **2**, 1378.

Mosse, H. L., Daniels, C. R. (1959), Linear Dyslexia. A New Form of Reading Disorder, *Amer. J. Psychother.*, **13**, 826–841.

Muller, R. G. E. (1960), Die visuelle Erfassung von Buchstaben bei legasthenischen Schulkindern, *Psychol. Beitr.*, **5**, 416–427.

Nadoleczny, M. (1913), Uber die Unfähigkeit lesen zu lernen (sogenannte kongenitale Wortblindheit) und ihre Beziehung zu Sprachstörungen, *Monat. Kinderh.*, **12** (Referate) 336–340.

Namnum, A., Prelinger, E. (1961), On the Psychology of the Reading Process, *Amer. J. Orthopsych.*, **31**, 820–828.

Nettleship, E. (1901), Cases of Congenital Word-blindness (Inability to Learn to Read), *Ophthal. Rev.*, **20**, 61–67.

Newbrough, J. R., Kelly, J. G. (1962), A Study of Reading Achievement in a Population of School-children, in *Reading Disability*, ed. J. Money, Baltimore, John Hopkins Press, pp. 61–72.

Nicholls, J. V. V. (1959), The Office Management of Patients with Reading Difficulties, *Canad. Med. Assoc. J.*, **81**, 356–360.

Nicholls, J. V. V. (1960), Congenital Dyslexia: a Problem in Aetiology, *Canad. med. ass. J.*, **82**, 575–579.

Norrie, E. (1939), *Om Ordblindhed*, Copenhagen.

Norrie, E. (1951), Ord-, tal- og nodenblindhed. Musikpaedagogen.

Norrie, E. (1954), Ordblindhedens (dyslexiens) arvegang, *Laesepaedagogen*, **2**, 61.

Ombredane, A. (1937), Le mechanisme et la correction des difficultés de la lecture connues sous le nom de cecité verbale congénitale, *Rapp. Psych. Schol. ler. Cong. Psych. Inf.*, Paris, 201–233.

Opitz, R. (1913), Einige Fälle von Wortblindheit, *Arch. Padogog.*, **2**, 79.

Orton, J. L. (1957), The Orton Story, *Bull. Orton Soc.*, **7**, 5–8.

Orton, S. T. (1925), Word-blindness' in School-children, *Arch. neur. psych.*, **14**, 581–615.

Orton, S. T. (1928), Specific Reading Disability—Strephosymbolia, *J. Amer. Med. Ass.*, **90**, 1095–1099.

Orton, S. T. (1928), An Impediment in Learning to Read—a Neurological Explanation of the Reading Disability, *School & Soc.*, 286–290.

Orton, S. T. (1934), Some Studies in Language Function, *Res. Publ. Ass. Res. Nerv. Ment. Dis.*, **13**, 614–633.

Orton, S. T. (1937), *Reading, Writing and Speech Problems in Children*, London, Chapman & Hall.

Orton, S. T. (1943), Visual Functions in Strephosymbolia, *Arch. Ophth.*, **30**, 707–717.

O'Sullivan, M. A., Pryles, C. U. (1962), Reading Disability in Children, *J. Pediat.*, **60**, 360–375.

Park, G. E. (1953), Mirror and Reversed Reading, *J. Pediat.*, **42**, 120–128.

Park, G. E. (1959), Medical Aspects of Reading Failures in Intelligent Children, *Sight-sav. Rev.*, **29**, 213–218.

Peters, A. (1908), Uber kongenitale Wortblindheir, *Munch. med. Woch.*, **55**, 1116 and 1239.

Peters, W. (1926), Psychologische Untersuchungen über Lesedefekte, *Zeit. Padagog. Psychol.*, **27**, 31–45.

Petty, L. (1960), A Normative Study of Reading Difficulty in Delinquents, *Delaware St. med. J.*, **32**, 24–26.

Petty, M. C. (1939), An Experimental Study of Certain Factors Influencing Reading Readiness, *J. Educ. Psychol.*, **30**, 215–230.

Pflugfelder, G. (1948), Psychologische Analyse eines Fall von angeborener Lese- u. Schreibschwäche, *Monat. Psych. Neur.*, **115**, 55–79.

Pintner, R. (1913), Inner Speech During Silent Reading, *Psychol. Rev.*, **20**, 129–157.
Plate, E. (1909), Vier Fälle von kongenitaler Wortblindheit in einer Familie, *Münch. med. Woch.*, **56**, 1793.
Prechtl, H. F. R. (1962), Reading Difficulties as a Neurological Problem in Child-hood, in *Reading Disability*, ed. J. Money. Baltimore, John Hopkins Press, pp. 187–193.
Prechtl, H. F. R., Stemmer, J. C. (1959), Ein choreatiformes Syndrom bei Kindern, *Wien. med. Woch.*, **109**, 461–463.
Prechtl, H. F. R., Stemmer, J. C. (1962), The Choreiform Syndrome in Children, *Dev. Med. Child Neur.*, **4**, 119–127.
Pritchard, E. (1911), Intermittent Word-blindness, *The Ophthalmosc.*, **9**, 171–172.
Rabinovitch, R. D. (1959), Reading and Learning Disabilities, being Chap. 43 in *Amer. Handb. Psych.*, Edit. Arieti, Vol. 1, Basic Books Inc., New York, pp. 857–869.
Rabinovitch, R. D. (1962), Dyslexia: Psychiatric Considerations, in *Reading Disability*, ed. J. Money. Baltimore, John Hopkins Press.
Rabinovitch, R. D., Drew, A. L., De Jong, R. N., Ingram, W., Withey, L. (1954), A Research Approach to Reading Retardation, in Neurology and Psychiatry in Childhood, *Res. Publ. Ass. nerv. ment. Dis.*, **34**, 363–396.
Rabkin, J. (1956), Reading Disability in Children, *S. Afr. med. J.*, **30**, 678–681.
Ranschburg, P. (1916), Die Leseschwäche (Legasthenie) und Rechenschwäche (Arithemie), der Kinder im Lichte des Experiments, *Abh. aus. d. Grenzgeb. Päd. Med.*, Berlin.
Ranschburg, P. (1925), Psychopathologie der Störungen des Lesens, Schreibens und Rechnens im Schulkindesalter, *Ber. uber d. 2, Kongr. Heilpäd im Munchen*, Springer, Berlin.
Ranschburg, P. (1927), Zur Pathophysiologie der Sprech-, Lese-, Schreib- und Druckfehler, *Psych. neur. Woch.*, **29**, 19–20.
Ranschburg, P. (1928), *Die Lese- u. Schreibstörungen des Kindesalters*, Halle, Marhold.
Reinhold, M. (1962), The Diagnosis of Congenital Dyslexia, in *Word-blindness or Specific Developmental Dyslexia*, ed. E. W. Franklin, London, Pitman Med. Publ. Co. Ltd., pp. 70–73.
Reinhold, M. (1963), The Effect of Laterality on Reading and Writing, *Proc. Roy. Soc. Med.*, **56**, 203–206.
Rémond, A., Gabersek, V. (1956), Lunettes pour l'enregistrement des électro-oculogrammes, *Rev. neur.*, **94**, 847–848.
Rémond, A., Gabersek, V. (1956), Technique et méthode d'enregistrement des mouvements des yeus en clinique neurologique. Application à l'étude de la lecture, *Rev. neur.*, **95**, 506–509.
Rémond, A., Gabersek, V. (1956), Les cheminements du regard au cours de la lecture. I. Les mouvements des yeux, *Rev. neur.*, **95**, 510–516.
Rémond, A., Gabersek, V. (1956), Les cheminements du regard au cours de la lecture. II. Les stations du regard, *Rev. neur.*, **95**, 516–521.
Rémond, A., Gabersek, V., Lesèvre, N. (1956), Corps d'oeil sur l'efficacité du regard dans la lecture, *Rev. neur.*, **95**, 455–470.
Rémond, A., Lesèvre, N., Gabersek, V. (1957), Approche d'une sémeiologie électro-graphique du regard, *Rev. neur.*, **96**, 536–546.
Riis-Vestergaard, I. (1962), Treatment at the Word-blind Institute, Copenhagen, in *Word-blindness or Specific Developmental Dyslexia*, ed. E. W. Franklin. London, Pitman Med. Publ. Co. Ltd., pp. 15–22.
Robinson, H. (1937), The Study of Disabilities in *Elem. School Reading, J.*, **38**, 1–14.
Robinson, H. M. (1946), *Why Pupils Fail in Reading*, Chicago, Univ. Chic. Press.
Rønne, H. (1936), Congenital Word-blindness in School-children, *Tr. Oph. Soc. U.K.*, **56**, 311–333.
Rønne, H. (1937), Medfødte Laesevanskligheder hos Skolebørn, *Ugesk. f. Laeger*, **9**, 185–192.
Rønne, H. (1943), Medicinske og paedagogiske problemer i ordblindesagen, *Social-paedagog. tidsskr.*, **3**, 121.
Rosenberg, M. E. (1961), A Brief Look at the State of Reading Retardation, *Labor Rep. No. 1, Commun. Projects Sect., Ment. Health Study Center.*

134   The dyslexic child

Roundinesco, Trélat, J. (1950), Note sur la dyslexie, *Bull. Soc. méd. Hôp. Paris,* •
    66, 1451–1458.
Runge (1926), Uber die sogenannt. kongenitale Wortblindheit, *Zlbl. Neur. Psych.,*
    42, 813–814.
Rutherfurd, W. J. (1909), The Aetiology of Congenital Word-blindness, with an
    Example, *Brit. J. Child. Dis.,* 6, 484–488.
Schilder, P. (1944), Congenital Alexia and its Relation to Optic Perception, *J. genet.
    psychol.,* 65, 67–88.
Schiøler, E. (1952), Ordblindhed-lidt om diagnose og undervisningsmetoder,
    Paedagog.-psykolog. tidskr., 12, 24.
Schlossman, A. (1960), Reading Difficulties in Children, *Eye, Ear, Nose, Thr. Monthly,*
    39, 514–518.
Schmitt, C. (1918), Developmental Alexia, *Elem. School J.,* 18, 680–700.
Schonell, F. J. (1945), *The Psychology of Teaching Reading,* Edinburgh and London,
    Oliver & Boyd.
Schonell, F. J. (1948), *Backwardness in the Basic Subjects,* 4th Edit., Edinburgh and
    London, Oliver & Boyd.
Schrock, R. (1912), Uber kongenitale Wortblindheit, Rats-u. Univ. Buchdruckerei
    Adlers Erbent Rostock.
Schwalbe-Hansen, P. A. (1937), Om "Ordblinde" Børn, *Ugesk. f. Lager.,* 99, 520–
    522.
de Séchelles (1962), The Treatment of Word-blindness, in *Word-blindness or Specific
    Developmental Dyslexia,* ed. E. W. Franklin. London, Pitman Med. Publ.
    Co. Ltd., pp. 23–27.
Sédan, J. (1951), Arithmo-alexie congénitale, *Rev. d'oto-neuro-ophtal.,* 23, 118–
    120.
Seymour, P. J. (1959), Efficient Reading, *Amer. orthop. J.,* 9, 73–76.
Shankweiler, D. P. (1962), Some Critical Issues Concerning Developmental Dyslexia,
    in *Word-blindness or Specific Developmental Dyslexia,* ed. E. W. Franklin.
    London, Pitman Med. Publ. Co. Ltd., pp. 51–55.
Sharp, P. (1956), Teaching the Strephosymbolie at the High School Level, *Bull.
    Orton Soc.,* 6, 20–22.
Sheldon, W., Hubble, D. V. (1960–61), Educational Problems in Children, *Trans.
    Hunterian Soc.,* 19, 106–128.
Shepherd, E. M. (1956), Reading Efficiency of 809 Average School-children. *Amer.
    J. Oph.,* 41, 1029–1039.
Silver, A. A., Hagin, R. (1960), Specific Reading Disability: Delineation of the
    Syndrome and Relationship to Cerebral Dominance, *Compreh. psych.,* 1,
    126–134.
Sinclair, A. H. (1948), Developmental Aphasia, *Brit. J. Ophth.,* 32, 522–531.
Skydsgaard, H. B. (1942), *Den konstitutionelle dyslexi,* Copenhagen.
Skydsgaard, H. B. (1944), Dyslexiens prognose, *Skolehyg. tidskr.*
Smith, D. E. P., Carrigan, P. M. (1959), *The Nature of Reading Disability,* New York,
    Harcourt, Brace & Co.
Solms, H. (1947), Beitrag zur Lehre von der sog. kongenitalen Wortblindheit,
    Monat. Psych. Neur., 115, 1–54.
Spiel, W. (1953), Beitrag zur kongenitalen Lese- und Schreibstörung, *Wien. Zeit.
    Nervenh. u. Grenzgeb.,* 7, 20–35.
Statten, T. (1953), Behaviour Patterns, Reading Disabilities, and EEG Findings,
    Amer. J. Psych., 110, 205–206.
Steen, S. W. (1958), Lesevansker hos barn og øyeundersøkelse av barn, *T. norske
    Laegeforen.,* 78, 186–187.
Stephenson, S. (1907), Six Cases of Congenital Word-blindness Affecting Three
    Generations of One Family, *The Ophthalmoscope,* 5, 482–484.
Stewart, R. E. (1950), Personality Maladjustment and Reading Achievement, *Amer.
    J. Orthopsych.,* 20, 410–417.
Subirana, A., Corominas, J., Oller-Daurel a L. (1950), Las Afasias congenitas
    infantiles, *Actas Luso-esp. neur. psiq.,* 9, 14–25.
Sutherland, A. H. (1922), Correcting School Disabilities in Reading, *Elem. School J.,*
    23, 37–42.
Tamm, A. (1924), Undersokningar av i skolan efterblivna barn, *Hygeia,* 86, 673–
    706.

Bibliography

Tamm, A. (1927), Medfödd ordblindhet och därmed besläktade rubbningar i barnaaldern, *Svenska läk.-sällsk. handl.*, **53**, 143–155.
Tamm, A. (1927), Die angeborene Wortblindheit und verwandte Störungen bei Kindern, *Zeit. psychoanal. Pädagog.*, **1**, 329.
Tamm, A. (1943), Ordblindher hos barn, *Pedagog. skr.*, **5**, 179–180.
Taylor, E. A. (1957). The Spans: Perception, Apprehension and Recognition, *Amer. J. Ophth.*, **44**, 501–507.
Thomas, C. J. (1905), Congenital Word-blindness and its Treatment, *Ophthalmoscope*, **3**, 380–385.
Thomas, C. J. (1908), The Aphasias of Childhood and Educational Hygiene, *Publ. Health*, **21**, 90–100.
Thompson, L. J. (1956), Specific Reading Disability—Strephosymbolia. 1. Diagnosis, *Bull. Orton Soc.*, **6**, 3–9.
Tjossem, T. D., Hansem, T. J., Ripley, H. S. (1962), An Investigation of Reading Difficulty in Young Children, *Amer. J. Psychiat.*, **118**, 1104–1113.
Variot, G., Lecomte (1906), Un cas de typhbolexie congénitale (cécité congénitale verbale, *Gaz. Hôp.*, **79**, 1479–1481.
Vermeylen, G. (1930), Un trouble rare de l'evolution du langage chez un enfant de 8 ans, 10 *Cong. belge neur. psych. J. de Neur.*, **30**, 827–836.
Vernon, M. D. (1957), *Backwardness in Reading. A Study of its Nature and Origin*, Cambridge, Camb. Univ. Press.
Wall, W. D. (1945), Reading Backwardness Among Men in the Army (1), *Brit. J. Educ. Psych.*, **15**, 28–40.
Wall, W. D. (1946), Reading Backwardness Among Men in the Army (2), *Brit. J. Educ. Psych.*, **16**, 133–148.
Wallin, J. E. H. (1921), Congenital Word-blindness, *Lancet*, **1**, 890–892.
Walter, K. (1954), Beitrag zum Problem der angeborenen Schreib- Lese- Schwache, (Kongenital Wortblindheit), *Nervenarzt*, **25**, 146–154.
Walters, R. H., van Loan, M., Crofts, J. (1961), A Study of Reading Disability, *J. cons. Psych.*, **25**, 277–283.
Warburg, F. (1911), Uber die angeborene Wortblindheit und die Bedeutung ihrer Kenntines fur den Unterricht, *Zeit. Kinderforsch.*, **16**, 97.
Wawrik, M. (1931), Eine experimentell-psychologische Untersuchung uber zwei Falle von Leseschwäche, *Zeit. Kinderforsch.*, **38**, 462–515.
Witty, P. A., Kopel, D. (1936), Sinistral and Mixed Manual Ocular Behaviour in Reading Disability, *J. Educ. Psychol.*, **27**, 119–134.
Witty, P. A., Kopel, D. (1936), Factors Associated with the Etiology of Reading Disability, *J. Educ. Psychol.*, **27**, 222–230.
Witty, P. A., Kopel, D. (1936), Heterophoria and Reading Disability, *J. Educ. Psych.*, **27**, 222–230.
Witty, P. A., Kopel, D. (1936), Studies of Eye-muscle Imbalance and Poor Fusion in Reading Disability, *J. Educ. Psych.*, **27**, 663–671.
Wolfe, L. (1941), Differential Factors in Specific Reading Disability. (1) Laterality of Functions, *J. Genet. Psych.*, **58**, 45–56.
Wolff, G. (1916), Uber kongenitale Wortblindheit, *Cor. -Bl. f. schweiz. Arzte*, **46**, 237–238.
Wollnerr, M. H. B. (1958), Some European Research in Reading Disabilities, *Education*, **78**, 555–560.
Woody, C., Phillips, A. J. (1934), The Effects of Handedness on Reversals in Reading, *J. Educ. Res.*, **27**, 651–662.
Yedinack, J. G. (1949), A Study of the Linguistic Functioning of Children with Articulation and Reading Disabilities, *J. Genet. Psych.*, **74**, 23–59.
Zangwill, O. L. (1960), *Cerebral Dominance and its Relation to Psychological Function*, Edinburgh, Oliver & Boyd.
Zenner (1893), Ein Fall von Unfähigheit zu Lesen (Alexie), *Neur. Zlbl.*, **12**, 293–299.

Index